The deep feeling for bread is carefully expressed in this verse taken from a calligraphy exhibit. As you handle bread—mixing, kneading and shaping it—recall its wisdom.

Be gentle when you touch BREAD
Let it not be uncared for, unwanted
Too often bread is taken for granted.
There is such beauty in bread:
Beauty of sun and soil
Beauty of patient toil;
Wind and rain have caressed it
Christ often blest it
Be gentle when you touch BREAD.

(Author unknown.)

books designed with giving in mind

Salads & Casseroles
Kid's Party Book
Pressure Cooking
Food Processor Cookbook
Peanuts & Popcorn
Kid's Pets Book
Make It Ahead
    French Cooking
Soups & Stews
Crepes & Omelets
Microwave Cooking
Vegetable Cookbook
Kid's Arts and Crafts
Bread Baking

The Crockery Pot Cookbook
Kid's Garden Book
Classic Greek Cooking
The Compleat American
    Housewife 1776
Low Carbohydrate Cookbook
Kid's Cookbook
Italian
Cheese Guide & Cookbook
Miller's German
Quiche & Souffle
To My Daughter, With Love
Natural Foods
Chinese Vegetarian

The Jewish Cookbook
Working Couples
Mexican
Sunday Breakfast
Fisherman's Wharf Cookbook
Charcoal Cookbook
Ice Cream Cookbook
Hippo Hamburger
Blender Cookbook
The Wok, a Chinese Cookbook
Cast Iron Cookbook
Japanese Country
Fondue Cookbook

from nitty gritty productions

A toast:
 "To a heritage of worldly bakers.
May those who follow expand the tradition
And cherish its multi-faceted rewards."

Bread Baking

by LOU SEIBERT PAPPAS

Illustrated by MIKE NELSON

© Copyright 1975
Nitty Gritty Productions
Concord, California

A Nitty Gritty Book*
Published by
Nitty Gritty Productions
P. O. Box 5457
Concord, California 94524

*Nitty Gritty Books - Trademark
Owned by Nitty Gritty Productions
Concord, California

Library of Congress Cataloging in Publication Data

Pappas, Lou Seibert.
    Bread baking.

    Includes index.
    1.   Bread.   I.   Title.
TX769.P24   641.8!15   75-8615
ISBN 0-911954-12-0

Contents

Introduction

My love for bread baking stems from my heritage. My maternal Swedish great-grandparents owned a thriving *bakeriet* in Gothenberg, Sweden, at the turn-of-the-century. The sparkling windows were a showplace filled with golden brown tea rings, swirled cinnamon twists and family-style white and orange-rye loaves. There was delectable Spritsar, apple cakes and marzipan tarts, as well.

As a new bride in the Pacific Northwest Grammy Helgesson carried on the baking tradition, producing big panfuls of sugar-glazed cinnamon rolls and 6 to 8 plump white loaves at a time for her large family. The children would race home from school and cut "heels" to frost with freshly-churned butter and homemade wild berry jelly.

My German *Grossmutter* Seibert cloaked her granite dishpan of rising dough with a fur throw. Her breads were more robust in character, emphasizing the local Eastern Oregon stone-cut grains in dark and crusty rye, wholewheat and pumpernickel varieties along with her holiday specialty, an almond and honey-glazed Bienenstich.

My mother combines both legacies with her own knack for blending grains, deftly turning out countless varieties of whole grain breads, beautiful caramelized sticky rolls and orange-frosted brioche cakes in rich succession.

Now I carry on the tradition, interweaving the decorative breads from my husband's Greek background with my own. Yaya's glorious anise-scented Christopsomo and lemon-imbued Easter Tsoureki are now integral to our holiday celebrations. The many international breads sampled on our travels have since been perfected and savored at home.

Our family "baking tree" emphasizes how bread making is a composite of lore, love and skill—plus a touch of magic, perhaps—passed down through generations in homes throughout the world.

The sensual delight of producing a loaf of bread and sharing it with family or friends is a joyful and rewarding experience for all. Often I divide a piece of dough with my children. Shaping the Danish Kringler is their specialty. Their young hands revel in the soft, springy feel of dough. They love watching it balloon in size. And most of all, they cherish its warm goodness. The tantalizing aroma and delectable taste of freshly baked bread offer pleasures hard to surpass. Turning out an honest loaf is not difficult once you master a few basic techniques.

Bread baking dates back to the Stone Age. It began in earnest when man turned from a nomadic hunting life to a more settled existence which allowed for the cultivation of grain. The first bread was an unleavened wafer-thin cake, baked on hot stones. Next the Egyptians turned bread baking into a skilled craft. Their bread was leavened with yeast-rich foam scooped from the top of fermenting wines. Breads in variety were found in the tombs of the Pharohs. Some were flavored with camphor; others with sesame and poppy seeds. Much later the European baker was prized as an important tradesman. Today many view this skill as a satisfying means of self-expression and the art of bread baking is experiencing new popularity.

This collection of breads, garnered through family traditions and worldly travels, endeavors to introduce you to bread making or expand your repertoire if you are already a baker. I hope they bring you joy.

Lou Seibert Pappas
Portola Valley, California

3

Facts and Tips for Breadmakers

Ingredients

Flour. Wheat flour, the major ingredient in bread, contains a protein substance called gluten. When wheat flour is combined with liquid, then stirred and kneaded, the gluten stretches to form the elastic network that holds the gas bubbles formed by the yeast. White all-purpose flour is wheat flour. It is available both bleached and unbleached. The latter is preferable because it is a sturdier flour containing more gluten. Whole wheat flour has less gluten than white flour and whole wheat breads are generally heavier and smaller. Rice and soy flour have no gluten so are unsatisfactory by themselves for making yeast breads. Because the amount and quality of gluten are never exactly the same, the amount of flour needed will vary. Temperatures and humidity can also affect the absorption properties of flour and the time needed for beating and kneading will vary for the same reason. With a little experience, a breadmaker will learn to recognize when the mixture "feels" right.

Special grains and flours such as rye, cracked wheat, buckwheat, soybean, rice, corn meal and wheat germ all add variety, character and extra nutrition to breads. Most need to be combined with all-purpose flour because they lack enough gluten to effect a proper bread structure.

<u>Leavening.</u> Yeast, the leavening agent most commonly used in bread making, is a living plant which grows in warm, moist doughs. It gives off bubbles of gas, causing the dough to rise. Yeast comes in two forms, active dry and compressed, which produce equally good results when used in the conventional mixing method of dissolving the yeast in warm water (85° to 95° for compressed; 105° to 115° for active dry). Only the dry form can be used in the easy-mix method where it is mixed with part of the flour, then the liquid is added and the mixture beaten with an electric mixer. This method requires the water to be warmer, between 120° and 130°. The temperature for dissolving

compressed yeast should never be more than 85° to 95°. A word of caution—if the liquid used in dissolving the yeast or adding to yeast mixtures is too hot it will kill the yeast and the bread will not rise. A candy thermometer is the most accurate way of testing the water temperature. One package, about 1 tablespoon, of active dry yeast is interchangeable with one 0.6 ounce cake of compressed yeast. Active dry yeast is less perishable than the compressed cakes which must be refrigerated. To determine if a cake of yeast is usable, crumble it between your fingers. If it crumbles easily, it's still good.

Liquids. The kind of liquid used in bread making influences the final product. Milk gives a soft crust and creamy white crumb. Breads made with water have a crisper, thicker crust such as found in French bread. Unpasteurized milk needs to be scalded to destroy a particular enzyme which causes "gummy" bread. Pasteurized, evaporated or reconstituted dry milk need only be warmed enough to activate the yeast.

Sugar. Stimulates the yeast to produce gas, helps the crust to brown and adds flavor. The sugar is usually in granulated form, but brown sugar,

molasses or honey may be used.

<u>Fat</u>. Butter, margarine, cooking oil or vegetable shortening makes breads tender, gives them a soft silky crumb and aids in browning. They also add flavor.

<u>Salt</u>. Not only enhances flavor, but is necessary to control the growth of the yeast, making the dough rise more slowly for a better texture.

<u>Eggs</u>. Add a golden color and rich flavor and make the crumb fine and the crust tender.

<u>Nuts and Fruits</u>. Add flavor and variety, but slow the rising time.

8

Tips and Techniques

<u>Preliminary Mixing</u>. Strong beating should be done either with an electric mixer or by hand using a wooden spoon to develop the gluten. Either way, add half of the specified amount of flour and beat hard a few minutes before adding the remaining flour.

<u>Kneading</u>. Preferably do this on a board, but if necessary you may use a counter top or table. Sprinkle the surface lightly with flour and rub some on your hands. Shape the dough into a round ball and place on the floured surface. Using the heels of your hands, push the dough away with a rolling motion. Fold it toward you. Then turn the dough one quarter turn around. Continue the sequence of pushing, folding and turning, making a rhythmic motion. Repeat until the dough is smooth, satiny, elastic and no longer sticky, adding more flour when necessary. Allow at least 10 minutes for kneading hand-mixed doughs. The necessary kneading time is reduced if you use a heavy duty electric mixer, such as a Kitchen Aid or Robert Coupe. These mixers come equipped with dough hooks which actually do the kneading for you. To test if the dough is kneaded enough, make an indentation with your finger. The dough will spring back when it is kneaded enough. Ample kneading creates bread with a springy texture and maximum volume. Extra kneading does not harm the dough, but enhances it.

<u>Greasing the bowl</u>. Rub the bowl with a thin film of butter, margarine or oil

and turn the dough in it so it is greased on all sides. This prevents a crust from forming during rising.

Rising. Select a draft-free location for the dough to rise. An even temperature of about 80° to 85° is best for all but refrigerator-type doughs. If your kitchen is not warm enough, you can create a warm place in any of these ways:

Set the bowl of dough in a cold oven with a large pan of hot water beneath it.

Set the bowl of dough in an oven with the oven light on.

Heat an electric oven to warm, then turn the heat off. Place the bowl of dough in the oven with the door slightly open.

Testing. To tell when the dough has doubled, press two fingertips lightly 1/2 inch into the dough. If the indentation remains, the dough is ready for shaping.

Punching down. Push your fist into the center of the dough. Pull the edges of the dough to the center and turn dough over and turn out onto lightly floured surface. Knead a minute or two to remove air bubbles.

Shaping. For a loaf of bread start by dividing the dough as specified in the recipe. Shape into a smooth ball. Stretch top surface of the dough, pulling it underneath to make a taut, smooth surface. Tuck ends underneath.

Testing for lightness before baking. Touch lightly with a finger. It should feel "poppy"—light and springy.

Glazes. Just before baking, the risen dough is often brushed with a glaze to give it a special finish when it is baked. The various glazes include water, lightly beaten egg white, egg yolk beaten with 1 tablespoon milk or water, cornstarch mixed with water, and cream. Each results in a slightly different finish.

Baking. Preheat the oven. Allow ample room for the heat to circulate around the pans. If tops of loaves begin to over-brown, lay a piece of aluminum foil loosely over the top of each one. To test for doneness, tap or rap the top of the loaf with your knuckles. If it sounds hollow, it is done.

Cooling. As soon as the bread or rolls are baked, remove from pans to a wire cooling rack. When cool, package in plastic bags, tie securely, and store at room temperature or refrigerate or freeze.

<u>Freezing</u>. Breads freeze beautifully when packaged air-tight in plastic freezing bags or wrapped in foil and sealed with tape. Label and date the packages. To reheat, let thaw completely at room temperature, wrap in foil, and heat in a 350° F oven 20 to 30 minutes, or until thoroughly heated. It is wise to leave breads unfrosted if you plan to freeze them. Frost just before using.

Coping With Problems

<u>Bread</u> that doesn't rise. When bread dough refuses to rise after a considerable time span, what should you do? You've probably killed the yeast, perhaps by combining it with liquid that was too hot. The best solution is to dissolve 1 package of active dry yeast and 1 teaspoon sugar in 1/2 cup warm water (110°). Mix in 1/2 cup all-purpose flour. Let stand in a warm place for 10 minutes, or until spongy. Beat this mixture into the unrisen dough. Then knead in enough additional flour for correct consistency. Proceed as

usual by placing the dough in a warm spot to rise.

<u>Bread that over rises</u>. What should you do when the shaped loaves of dough have risen too much in the pans before they are baked. You can turn the dough out on a floured board, knead lightly and reshape into loaves. Place in greased pans and let rise again just until doubled, then bake.

<u>Punching down</u>. How often can you punch dough down before shaping it? It is quite all right to let the dough rise twice and punch it down twice before shaping it. Remember dough rises more quickly each successive time it rises and is punched down. It is important to punch the dough down as soon as it has doubled in size so the texture will be fine-grained, rather than coarse.

<u>No time to finish</u>. What should you do if you have mixed the dough and then are not free to complete the rising and baking sequence? Let the dough rise once, punch it down and refrigerate it, covered with plastic wrap. Later, either the same day or the following one, remove the pan from the refrigerator and let the dough rise in a warm place until doubled in size. Shape, let rise and bake.

13

Plain and Wholesome Loaves

15

BASIC WHITE BREAD

This wholesome bread is extremely versatile. Five delicious variations can be made from this basic recipe.

2 pkg. active dry yeast
1 cup warm water
1 cup milk
3 tbs. sugar
2-1/2 tsp. salt
3 tbs. butter
5 cups all-purpose flour
Egg Glaze: 1 egg white beaten with 1 tbs. water

Sprinkle yeast into warm water. Let stand until dissolved. Heat milk. Pour into a large mixing bowl containing sugar, salt and butter. Cool to lukewarm. Stir in dissolved yeast. Add 3 cups flour. Beat 5 minutes. Gradually add enough remaining flour to make a soft dough. Turn out onto a lightly floured board. Knead until smooth and no longer sticky, about 10 minutes. Place in a greased bowl. Butter top of dough lightly. Cover with a clean kitchen towel and let rise in a warm place until doubled in size, about 1-1/2 hours. Punch dough down. Turn out onto a lightly floured board and knead gently a minute or two to remove air bubbles. Divide in half and shape into loaves. Place in 2 greased 9 x 5 inch loaf pans. (Or, divide each half into thirds. Roll each piece into a rope, and braid. Place on greased baking sheets and continue as directed for loaf pans.) Cover with a kitchen towel. Let rise in a warm place until doubled in size, about 45 minutes. Brush tops with Egg Glaze. Bake in 375° F oven 40 to 45 minutes, or until brown and loaves sound hollow when thumped. Makes 2 loaves or braids.

17

WHOLE WHEAT BREAD

Substitute 2-1/2 cups whole wheat flour and 1/4 cup wheat germ for 2-3/4 cups of the all-purpose flour specified above.

CINNAMON SWIRL BREAD

Let basic dough rise once. Punch down. Knead a minute or two on lightly floured board. Divide in half. Roll into 15 x 7-inch rectangles. Spread each one with 1 tablespoon soft butter. Combine 6 tablespoons sugar with 2 teaspoons cinnamon. Spread half of mixture on each rectangle. Roll tightly as for jelly roll, beginning with narrow side. Place in pans to rise in warm placed until almost double, about 35 to 40 minutes. Bake in 375° F oven 40 to 45 minutes or until done.

18

RAISIN BREAD

Follow basic recipe. After mixture has been beaten 5 minutes, stir in 1 cup raisins and enough remaining flour to make soft dough. Proceed as directed.

CHEDDAR CHEESE BREAD

Let basic dough rise once. Punch down. Knead in 1-1/2 cups grated, sharp Cheddar cheese. Divide in half. Shape into rounds. Place in two greased 9-inch round cake pans to rise in warm place until almost double, 35 to 40 minutes. Bake in 375° F oven 40 to 45 minutes.

19

FRENCH STYLE WHITE BREAD

Let basic dough rise once. Punch down. Knead lightly. Divide dough in half. Shape into two long loaves. Place on greased baking sheets. Let rise in warm place until doubled in size. Make diagonal slashes with a razor blade about 2-1/2 inches apart. Brush with water. Bake in 375° F oven 40 to 45 minutes or until done.

QUICK HONEY WHITE BREAD

This recipe goes together fast in rapid-mix style.

7 to 8 cups all-purpose flour
1 cup non-fat dry milk powder
3 pkg. active dry yeast
1 tbs. salt
3 cups warm water (125°)
1/3 cup soft butter or margarine
1/3 cup honey

Place 2 cups flour, milk powder, yeast, and salt in a large mixing bowl. Pour in water and beat 1 minute using an electric mixer. Add butter and honey. Beat 1 minute longer. Gradually add enough remaining flour to make a soft dough. Beat well, using a heavy duty electric mixer or wooden spoon. Turn out on a lightly floured board. Knead 5 to 10 minutes, or until smooth and satiny. Place in a greased bowl. Lightly butter top of dough. Cover with a clean kitchen towel. Let rise in a warm place until doubled in size, about 1-1/2 hours. Punch dough down. Turn out on a lightly floured board. Knead gently a minute or two to remove air bubbles. Divide into three pieces. Shape into loaves. Place in three greased 9 x 5-inch loaf pans. Cover with a clean kitchen towel. Let rise in a warm place until doubled in size, about 35 to 40 minutes. Bake in 375° F oven 40 to 45 minutes, or until golden brown and loaves sound hollow when thumped. Makes 3 loaves.

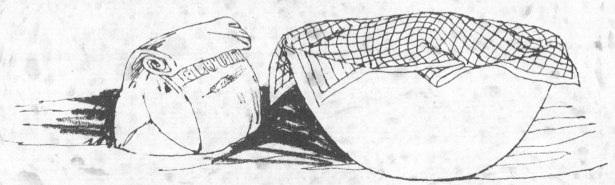

WHOLE WHEAT COFFEE CAN BREAD

Coffee cans make a neat round container for baking bread. The baked loaves come out of the cans with ease—simply turn them upside-down.

3 cups unbleached all-purpose flour
3 cups whole wheat flour
1-1/2 tsp. salt
2 pkg. active dry yeast

2-1/2 cups warm water (125°)
1/4 cup brown sugar
1/4 cup butter

In a large mixing bowl stir together 1 cup unbleached flour, 1 cup wholewheat flour, salt, yeast, and brown sugar. Stir in water. Beat until smooth. Mix in butter and remaining wholewheat flour. Beat 5 minutes longer. Gradually add enough of the remaining all-purpose flour to make a stiff dough. Turn out on floured board. Knead 5 to 10 minutes, or until smooth and no longer sticky. Place in a greased bowl. Butter top of dough lightly. Cover with clean kitchen towel and let rise in warm place until doubled in size, about 1-1/2 hours. Punch down and turn out on a lightly floured board. Knead a minute or two to remove air bubbles. Divide in half and shape into 2 round loaves. Place in two greased 2-pound-size coffee cans or two greased 9 x 5-inch loaf pans. Cover with kitchen towel. Let rise until doubled, about 35 to 40 minutes. Bake at 375° F for 40 to 45 minutes, or until loaves sound hollow when thumped. Makes 2 loaves.

CHEESE WHEAT BREAD

Follow the recipe for Whole Wheat Coffee Can Bread except mix 1 tablespoon dried oregano and 2 cups shredded Cheddar or Swiss cheese into the dough after it has risen once. Continue as directed.

HEALTH BREAD

Follow the recipe for Whole Wheat Coffee Can Bread, except substitute 1/2 cup wheat germ for 1/2 cup all-purpose flour.

DATE PECAN BREAD

This spicy fruit bread is exceptional sliced and spread with natural cream cheese and orange marmalade.

2 pkg. active dry yeast
3 tbs. sugar
2-1/2 tsp. salt
2 tsp. grated orange peel
1/2 cup nonfat dried milk solids
1 cup unsifted whole wheat flour
5 cups all-purpose flour
2-3/4 cups warm water
3 tbs. soft butter
1 cup chopped, pitted dates
1/2 cup coarsely chopped pecans

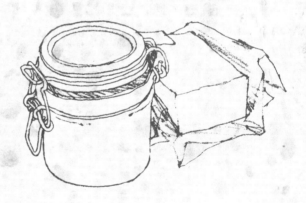

Place yeast, sugar, salt, orange peel, milk solids, whole wheat flour, and 1

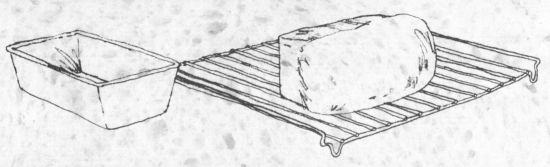

cup all-purpose flour in a large mixing bowl. Stir in very warm water (125°). Beat until smooth. Mix in butter and enough remaining flour to make a soft dough. Stir in dates and nuts. Turn out on a lightly floured board and knead until smooth. Place in a greased bowl. Cover and let rise in a warm spot until doubled in size. Turn out on a floured board and knead lightly. Divide dough in half and shape into 2 loaves. Place in 2 greased 9 x 5-inch loaf pans. Cover and let rise until doubled. Bake in a 375° F oven 35 to 40 minutes or until loaves sound hollow when thumped. Turn out and let cool on wire racks. Makes 2 loaves.

ANADAMA BREAD

This old-time New England corn meal bread is pleasantly sweet. It is especially good toasted and spread with marmalade or apple butter.

5 cups all-purpose flour	2 tsp. salt	1/2 cup molasses
1 cup corn meal	2 cups warm water (125°)	
2 pkg. active dry yeast	5 tbs. soft butter	

Stir 2 cups flour, corn meal, yeast and salt together in a mixing bowl. Add water, butter and molasses. Beat hard for 3 minutes. Mix in enough remaining flour to make a stiff dough. Turn out onto a floured board. Knead until no longer sticky. Place in a greased bowl. Butter top of dough lightly. Cover with a clean kitchen towel. Let rise in a warm place until doubled in size, about 1-1/2 hours. Punch dough down. Turn out onto floured board. Knead a minute or two. Divide dough in half. Shape into two balls. Place in greased 9 x 5-inch loaf pans. Cover. Let rise until doubled, about 35 to 40 minutes. Bake at 375° F 45 to 50 minutes, or until loaves sound hollow when tapped. Makes 2 loaves.

MIXED NUT BREAD

This bread slices beautifully, revealing the assorted nuts which stud each slice. It makes a stellar bread to offer with a cheese tray for dessert.

1 pkg. active dry yeast
1/4 cup warm water
3/4 cup milk
3 tbs. butter
3 tbs. sugar
1 tsp. salt
1 egg
2-3/4 cups all-purpose flour
3/4 cup roasted, salted mixed nuts (do not chop)
1 egg white, lightly beaten

Sprinkle yeast into warm water. Stir until dissolved. Heat milk. Pour over butter and sugar in a large mixing bowl. Let cool to lukewarm. Stir in salt, egg and dissolved yeast. Gradually add enough flour to make a soft dough. Beat well after each addition. Mix in nuts. Turn out onto a lightly floured board. Knead until smooth. Place in greased bowl. Butter top of dough lightly. Cover with a clean kitchen towel. Let rise in a warm place until doubled in size, about 1-1/2 hours. Punch dough down and turn out on a floured board. Knead a minute or two to remove air bubbles. Shape into a flat cake. Place in a greased 9-inch round cake pan. Cover. Let rise in a warm place until doubled, about 35 to 40 minutes. Brush with beaten egg white. Bake in 350° F oven 35 to 40 minutes, or until loaf sounds hollow when thumped. Makes 1 loaf.

PEASANT POTATO ROUNDS

Mashed potatoes keep bread moist and make it age well.

1 pkg. active dry yeast
1-1/4 cups warm water
1-1/2 cups rye flour
3/4 tsp. salt
1/4 cup molasses
1 cup mashed potatoes
1 tbs. caraway seeds
1-3/4 cups all-purpose flour
Cornstarch Glaze

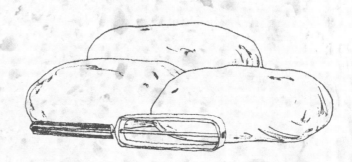

30

Sprinkle yeast into 1/4 cup warm water. Let stand until dissolved. Add remaining 1 cup water, 1 cup rye flour, salt, molasses, potatoes and caraway seed. Beat well. Gradually add 1 cup all-purpose flour and remaining rye flour. Beat until smooth. Beat in enough all-purpose flour to make a soft dough.

Turn out on a lightly floured board. Knead in remaining flour. Place in a greased bowl. Butter top of dough lightly. Cover with a clean kitchen towel. Let rise in a warm place until doubled in size, about 1-1/2 hours. Punch down. Turn out on a floured board. Knead a minute or two. Shape into one large round. Place in a greased 9-inch round pan or casserole. Cover. Let rise in a warm place until doubled in size, about 35 to 40 minutes. Bake at 375° F 40 to 45 minutes. Brush with Cornstarch Glaze the last 10 minutes of baking. The loaf should sound hollow when baked. Makes 1 loaf.

Cornstarch Glaze: Bring 1/4 cup water to a boil. Blend in 1 teaspoon cornstarch which has been mixed with 1 tablespoon cold water. Boil, stirring constantly, until thickened.

31

GRAMMY'S ORANGE BREAD

Shreds of orange rind punctuate this wholesome four-grain bread.

2-1/2 cups water
1 cup oatmeal
2 pkg. active dry yeast
2-1/2 tsp. salt
peel from 1 orange
1/3 cup butter
1/4 cup molasses
1 cup warm milk
1-1/2 cups barley flour
1 cup rye flour
3 to 4 cups all-purpose flour

32

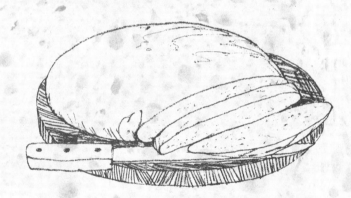

Place 2 cups water and oatmeal in a saucepan. Bring to a boil and boil 1

minute. Turn into a large mixing bowl. Let cool to lukewarm. Sprinkle yeast into the remaining 1/2 cup warm water. Let stand until dissolved. Scrape white pith from orange rind with a spoon. Place rind in a blender container with 2 tablespoons water. Blend until finely chopped. Add yeast, salt, chopped orange peel, butter and molasses to oatmeal mixture. Stir in warm milk. Gradually add barley, rye and white flours. Mix to make a soft dough. Turn out on a lightly floured board. Knead until smooth and elastic. Place in a large greased bowl. Butter the top lightly. Cover with a clean kitchen towel. Let rise until doubled in size, about 1-1/2 hours. Punch dough down. Knead to remove air bubbles. Divide in 3 parts. Shape into loaves. Place in greased 9 x 5-inch loaf pans or shape into round loaves and place on a greased baking sheet. Cover and let rise until doubled in size, about 35 to 40 minutes. Bake in a 375° F oven 35 to 40 minutes, or until the loaves sound hollow when thumped. Makes 3 loaves.

RUSSIAN BLACK BREAD

Slices of this rich dark loaf are superb spread with cream cheese and lox.

1-3/4 cups rye flour
1-3/4 cups all-purpose flour
1 tbs. brown sugar
1 tsp. salt
1 cup all-bran cereal
1 tbs. caraway seed, crushed
1/2 tsp. fennel seed, crushed
1-1/2 tsp. instant coffee powder

1 pkg. active dry yeast
1-1/4 cups water
2 tbs. cider vinegar
3 tbs. dark molasses
1/2 oz. (1/2 square)
    unsweetened chocolate
3 tbs. butter
Cornstarch Glaze

34

Place 1/2 cup rye flour, 3/4 cup all-purpose flour, brown sugar, salt, cereal, caraway seed, fennel seed, coffee powder and yeast in a large mixing bowl. Stir to blend. Heat water, vinegar, molasses, chocolate and butter together until liquids are very warm (about 125°). Gradually add to dry ingredients. Beat well 2 minutes. Gradually add enough of the remaining rye and all-purpose flours to make a soft dough. Turn out onto a lightly floured board. Knead until smooth and elastic. Place in a greased bowl. Butter top of dough lightly. Cover with a clean kitchen towel. Let rise in a warm place until doubled in size, about 1-1/2 hours. Turn out onto a lightly floured board and knead a few times to remove air bubbles. Shape into a round loaf. Place in greased 8-inch round cake pan or on a greased baking sheet. Cover and let rise until doubled, about 30 to 40 minutes. Bake at 350° F 40 to 45 minutes, or until loaf sounds hollow when thumped. When bread is done, brush top with Cornstarch Glaze. Bake 2 to 3 minutes longer, or until glaze is set. Makes 1 loaf.

Cornstarch Glaze: Bring 1/4 cup water to boil. Blend in 1 teaspoon cornstarch which has been mixed with 1 tablespoon cold water. Boil until thickened, stirring constantly.

VARIETY BREAD

Assorted seasonings rolled inside this plain loaf make it extra special.

2 pkg. active dry yeast
2-1/2 cups warm water
1 tbs. sugar
5-1/2 to 6 cups unbleached flour
1 tbs. salt

2 tbs. oil
yellow cornmeal
Glaze: 1 egg white beaten
    with 1 tbs. water

36   Sprinkle yeast into warm water in mixing bowl. Stir in sugar until dissolved. Gradually beat in 3 cups flour, salt and oil until smooth. Add enough additional flour to make a soft dough. Turn out onto a floured board. Knead until smooth. Place in a greased bowl. Cover with a clean kitchen towel. Let rise in a warm place until doubled in size, about 1-1/2 hours. Punch dough down. Turn out onto floured board. Knead 2 to 3 minutes. Divide in half. Shape into two long, French-style loaves. Place on a baking sheet which has

been sprinkled with cornmeal. Cover. Let rise in a warm place 20 minutes. Slash diagonally with a razor blade. Brush with glaze. Bake in 400° F oven 35 to 40 minutes, or until loaves sound hollow when thumped. Makes 2 loaves.

Filled Loaves

Let the above dough rise once as directed. Punch down. Turn onto a lightly floured board. Knead a minute or two. Divide in half. Roll each half into a 10 x 14-inch rectangle. Sprinkle surface with one of the suggested fillings, or one of your own choice. Shape into loaves and proceed as directed.

37

Fillings:

1/2 cup crumbled crisp bacon and 3 tablespoons chopped green onion
1/2 cup shredded Parmesan cheese and 1 tablespoon dried oregano
1/4 cup chopped shallots
4 cloves garlic, finely chopped and blended with 2 tablespoons butter

Brioche and Egg Breads

39

BRIOCHE

Buttery egg breads are best served hot to release their flavor and make each morsel meltingly tender. This basic Brioche recipe can be used many ways.

1 pkg. active dry yeast
1/4 cup warm water
1/2 cup milk
1/2 cup butter
2 tbs. sugar
1/2 tsp. salt
3 eggs
1 egg yolk
3-1/4 cups all-purpose flour
Egg Glaze: 1 egg yolk beaten with 1 tbs. milk

Sprinkle yeast into warm water and stir until dissolved. Heat milk until warm. Beat butter until creamy. Add sugar, salt, whole eggs and egg yolk. Beat well.

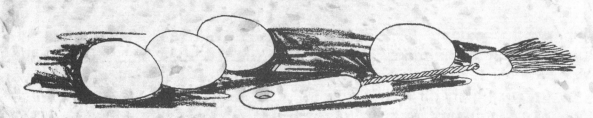

Add milk and yeast mixture. Gradually add just enough flour to make a soft dough. Beat well after each addition. Turn out on a lightly floured board. Knead until smooth and satiny. Place in a greased bowl. Butter top of dough lightly. Cover with a clean kitchen towel. Let rise in a warm place until doubled in size. Turn out on a lightly floured board and knead lightly. Cut off 1/5 of the dough for the top-knot. Shape remaining dough into a ball. Place in a greased 2-quart brioche pan. Cut an X in the center with scissors or a sharp knife. Shape reserved dough into a tear-drop. Place point down in the X. Cover. Let rise until doubled in size. Brush with egg glaze. Bake in 375° F oven 30 to 35 minutes, or until loaf sounds hollow when thumped. Serve warm. Makes 1 large loaf.

41

BRIOCHE BRAID

Prepare Brioche dough as directed on page 40. Let rise in a warm place until doubled, about 1-1/2 hours. Turn out on a floured board and knead lightly. Divide dough into three pieces. Roll into ropes about 14 inches long. Braid on a greased baking sheet. Cover with a kitchen towel. Let rise until doubled, about 35 to 40 minutes. Brush with Egg Glaze. Sprinkle with poppy or sesame seeds. Bake in 350° F oven 30 to 35 minutes, or until golden brown. Makes 1 large braid.

BRIOCHE CHEESE BRAID

42

Prepare Brioche dough as directed on page 40. Let rise in a warm place until doubled in size, about 1-1/2 hours. Turn out on a floured board. Knead 1-1/2 cups diced or shredded Bonbel or Samsoe cheese into the dough. Divide into three pieces. Roll into ropes about 14 inches long. Braid dough on a greased baking sheet. Cover with a kitchen towel. Let rise in a warm place until doubled in size. Bake as directed for Brioche Braid.

SAUSAGE IN BRIOCHE

Prepare Brioche dough as directed on page 40. Let dough rise in a warm place until doubled in size. Punch down. Chill 1 hour or longer for easier handling. Have cooked sausage ready—Simmer 10 to 12 mild Italian sausages (about 3 pounds) for 20 minutes and chill. Or simmer 2 Italian coteghino sausages (about 3 pounds) for 40 minutes and chill. For the small sausages, divide the dough into 10 to 12 pieces. For the large sausages, divide dough in half. Roll pieces of dough into rectangles about 1/4 inch thick. Place a sausage along one side of each rectangle. Roll up, encasing with dough. Place rolls seam side down on a greased baking sheet. Pinch in the ends. Use small aspic cutters to cut out crescents, stars or hearts from dough scraps. Place on top of rolls. Cover with kitchen towel. Let rise in warm place 20 minutes. Brush with Egg Glaze. Bake in 375° F oven 20 minutes or until nicely browned. Serve as an entree or slice and serve as appetizers. Makes 10 to 12 entree servings or 4 to 5 dozen appetizers.

43

CHEESE IN BRIOCHE

Prepare Brioche dough as directed on page 40. Let rise in a warm place until doubled in size. Punch down. Chill dough 1 hour or longer for easier handling. Divide into 12 pieces. Roll each into a rectangle about 1/4 inch thick. Sprinkle each rectangle with 1/3 cup grated Gruyere or Swiss cheese. Roll up like a jelly roll. Decorate the top of each with designs cut from dough scraps. Let stand 10 minutes. Brush with Egg Glaze. Bake in 375° F oven 20 minutes or until browned. Slice and serve hot. Makes 48 to 60 appetizers.

BRIOCHE FILBERT ROUNDS

Prepare Brioche dough as directed on page 40. Let rise in a warm place until doubled, about 1-1/2 hours. Turn out onto a floured board. Knead in 1/2 cup coarsely chopped, toasted filberts. Divide dough in half. Shape into balls. Place in two well-buttered, tall juice cans (46 oz. size). Cover. Let rise in a warm place until doubled. Bake in a 350° F oven 35 minutes or until loaves sound hollow when thumped. Turn out of cans. Cool on racks. Makes 2 round loaves.

BRIOCHE MOUSSELINE

Here is a richer version of the basic Brioche, which is ideal for fancy sandwiches and desserts.

1 pkg. active dry yeast	1/4 cup sugar
1/4 cup warm water	1 tsp. salt
1/4 cup warm milk	8 eggs
1 cup butter	4 cups all-purpose flour

Sprinkle yeast into warm water. Stir until dissolved. Cream butter. Beat in sugar, salt and eggs well. Add warm milk and dissolved yeast. Gradually add flour. Beat well. This dough will be too soft to knead. Cover with a kitchen towel. Let rise until doubled. Stir down. Turn into a greased 10-inch tube pan. Let rise in warm place until doubled. Bake in 375° F oven 45 minutes. Makes 1 large ring.

BRIOCHE ONION SANDWICHES

Cut a Brioche Mousseline in thin slices. If desired, cut a 3-inch round from each slice. Blanch 2 sweet red onions in water to cover for 3 minutes. Drain. Peel and slice very thin. Spread sandwiches with mayonnaise (preferably homemade). Top with onion slices. Dip edges of sandwiches in mayonnaise and then in finely chopped parsley. Cover. Chill until serving time.

BRIOCHE WITH CHOCOLATE SAUCE

46 Cut Brioche Mousseline in wedges or rounds. Cover each slice with a spoonful of whipped cream or vanilla ice cream. Top with Chocolate Sauce. Decorate with whipped cream.

Chocolate Sauce: Heat together 6 ounces semi-sweet chocolate, 1/4 cup light corn syrup, 1/2 cup light cream or strong coffee and 1-1/2 tablespoons brandy or Cognac. Use as directed.

BRIOCHE RING

Glaze this lovely bread with apricot preserves and serve with fresh fruit, Cointreau-laced orange sauce and whipped cream.

1 pkg. active dry yeast
1/4 cup warm water
1-1/2 cups all-purpose flour
1 tbs. sugar

1 tsp. salt
2 eggs
1/2 cup soft butter

Sprinkle yeast into warm water. Let stand until dissolved. Mix flour, sugar, salt, eggs and dissolved yeast together. Beat until smooth. Beat in butter, 1 tablespoon at a time. Dough will be too soft to knead. Cover and let rise in warm place until doubled in size. Punch down. Turn into a greased 1-1/2 quart ring mold. Cover. Let rise until doubled in size. Bake in a 375° F oven for 25 minutes, or until golden brown. Cool slightly on a cake rack, then turn out of pan. Makes 1 ring.

DESSERT BRIOCHE WITH FRUIT

Bake a Brioche Ring as directed. Cool. Bring 1/2 cup apricot preserves and 1 tablespoon brandy to a boil. Force through a sieve to make a smooth sauce. Brush top of ring with apricot glaze. Place on a serving plate. Encircle with apricot halves and bunches of seedless grapes or fresh strawberries. Pass ice cream balls or whipped cream which has been flavored with kirsch or Cointreau, and Orange Syrup.

Orange Syrup: Mix 1/2 cup sugar and 1/2 cup water together in a small saucepan. Cook until dissolved. Stir in 1/2 cup orange juice or 1/4 cup each Cointreau and brandy.

BRIOCHE SANDWICH STAR

This spectacular star-shaped brioche might adorn a party buffet table. It is designed to be filled with assorted finger sandwiches or strips of steak.

1 pkg. active dry yeast
1/4 cup warm water
1/2 cup butter
2 tbs. sugar
1 tsp. salt
1/4 cup brandy, sherry or water
4 eggs
3-1/4 cups all-purpose flour
Egg Glaze: 1 egg yolk beaten with 1 tbs. milk

Sprinkle yeast into warm water. Let stand until dissolved. Cream butter. Beat in sugar, salt and brandy, sherry or water. Add eggs one at a time. Beat well. Add 1 cup flour. Beat well. Stir in dissolved yeast. Gradually add remaining flour, beating well after each addition. Turn out on a floured board. Knead until smooth and satiny. Place in a lightly greased bowl. Cover with a kitchen towel. Let rise in a warm place until doubled in size, about 1-1/2 hours. Turn out onto a lightly floured board. Knead to release air bubbles. Roll into a 14 inch circle. Place on a greased 14-inch pizza pan. With a sharp-pointed knife cut star points, about 2-1/2 inches long, around the outer edge. Make about 12 to 14 points in all. Shape remaining dough into a ball. Roll into a 9 inch circle. Place in the center of the star. Cover and let rise in a warm place until doubled in size. Brush with Egg Glaze. Bake in a 375° F oven 30 minutes or until golden brown and loaf sounds hollow when thumped. Let cool on a cake rack. Makes 1 large Brioche star.

51

Brioche Star pictured on page 7.

continued

Filling Suggestions for Brioche Star

Assorted Sandwiches: With a serrated knife, slice off the center top layer of the Brioche Star. Hollow out the middle, removing the bread in one piece. Slice it to make triangular sandwiches, using an assortment of fillings such as ham, egg salad, crab, smoked salmon, cream cheese and watercress, toasted almond or olive and cream cheese. Fit triangle sandwiches back into hollowed out center. Replace top layer and serve.

Steak Sandwich: Cut top off of Brioche Star and cut out the center section. Blend together 2 tablespoons soft butter, 1 minced shallot, 2 teaspoons minced parsley, 1/2 teaspoon grated lemon peel and 1 clove minced garlic. Spread cut surfaces of hollowed out center with the seasoned butter. Heat loaf in a 350° F oven 10 minutes, or until hot through. Meanwhile, pan fry a 1-1/2 pound top round or sirloin steak in 1 tablespoon butter. Turn to brown both sides. Cook medium rare. Remove from pan. Slice into very thin strips. Place strips inside of star. Replace top. Cut into pie-shaped wedges to serve. Makes 8 servings.

52

SALLY LUNN

This renowned Southern bread looks festive baked in a fluted tube pan.

1 pkg. active dry yeast
1/2 cup warm water
1 cup warm milk
1/2 cup soft butter

1/4 cup sugar
1-1/2 tsp. salt
4-1/2 to 5 cups all-purpose flour
3 eggs

Sprinkle yeast into warm water in a large mixing bowl. Let stand until dissolved. Add milk, butter, sugar, salt and 1 cup of the flour. Beat until smooth. Add eggs one at a time. Beat well after each addition. Gradually add enough remaining flour to make a soft dough. (The dough is too soft to knead). Place in a greased bowl. Cover with a kitchen towel. Let rise until doubled in size, about 1-1/2 hours. Stir dough down. Spoon into a greased 10 inch tube pan or kugelhopf mold. Cover and let rise until doubled, about 45 minutes. Bake in 375° F oven 35 to 40 minutes, or until loaf sounds hollow when thumped. Makes 1 large bread ring.

53

MONKEY BREAD

Serving this bread is great fun. The butter-dipped rolls pull apart with ease from the big handsome ring.

1 pkg. active dry yeast
1/4 cup warm water
1 cup milk
1 cup butter
2 tbs. sugar
3 eggs
54 1 tsp. salt
4 cups all-purpose flour

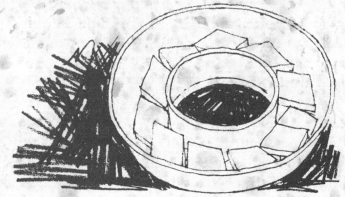

Sprinkle yeast into warm water. Let stand until dissolved. Heat milk and 1/2 cup butter together until warm. Pour into a mixing bowl. Add sugar and eggs. Beat until smooth. Stir in dissolved yeast mixture and salt. Add 1 cup flour. Beat until smooth. Gradually add enough of the remaining flour to make a soft dough. Turn out on lightly floured board. Knead until smooth and satiny. Place in a greased bowl. Butter top of dough lightly. Cover with a clean kitchen towel. Let rise in a warm place until doubled in size. Punch dough down. Turn out on a lightly floured board. Knead lightly. Melt remaining butter. Roll dough out on floured board until about 1/3 inch thick. Using a 2-1/2 inch round cookie cutter or a diamond-shaped cookie cutter, cut dough into rounds or diamonds. Roll and cut scraps until all dough is used. Dip each piece in butter to coat both sides. Place in overlapping layers in a greased 10-inch ring mold (3 quart size). Cover pan with a towel. Place in a warm place to rise, about 45 minutes. Bake in 350° F oven 35 minutes or until nicely browned and loaf sounds hollow when thumped. Turn out on large plate and serve while warm. Or, let cool, wrap air-tight and freeze. Allow to thaw and reheat before serving. Makes 1 ring.

DILL BATTER BREAD

Fragrant dill seeds crunch in this cheese-streaked round loaf.

1 pkg. active dry yeast
3 cups all-purpose flour
2 tbs. <u>each</u> sugar and dill seed
1 tsp. salt
1-1/4 cups very warm water

1/3 cup softened butter
2 eggs
1 cup (4 oz.) shredded Cheddar
<u>or</u> Monterey Jack cheese

56   Place yeast, 1 cup flour, sugar, dill seed and salt in a large mixing bowl. Pour in water and beat until smooth. Add butter and eggs. Beat until blended. Gradually add remaining flour. Beat well. Mix in cheese. Cover and let rise in a warm place until doubled. Stir down. Turn into a greased 2-quart souffle dish, fondue dish or casserole. Cover. Let rise until doubled, about 45 minutes. Bake in 350° F oven 1 hour or until loaf sounds hollow when thumped. Makes 1 round loaf.

ITALIAN PARMESAN BREAD

This mushroom-shaped loaf, streaked with cheese, is a fine companion to an Italian dinner.

1 pkg. active dry yeast
3/4 cup warm water
2 tbs. sugar
1 tsp. salt
3 cups all-purpose flour
4 eggs
1/2 cup soft butter
1 cup freshly grated Parmesan cheese
1 cup shredded Monterey Jack cheese
1 tsp. dried oregano (optional)

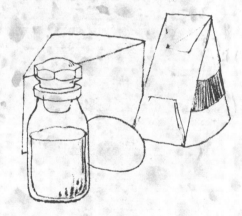

58

Sprinkle yeast into warm water in a large mixing bowl. Let stand until dissolved. Add sugar, salt, and 1 cup of the flour. Beat well. Add 3 eggs one at a time. Beat until smooth. Beat in butter. Gradually add enough remaining flour to make a soft dough. Turn out on floured board. Knead until smooth and satiny. Place in a greased bowl. Butter top of dough lightly. Cover with a kitchen towel. Let rise in a warm place until doubled in size. Turn out on a floured board. Knead lightly. Roll out into a rectangle about 10 to 16 inches. Beat remaining egg. Blend in cheeses and oregano. Spread cheese filling over dough. Roll up firmly from narrow end. Shape into a round by folding ends underneath. Place in a greased 2 quart round baking dish (preferably one with straight sides about 3 inches high, such as a souffle or fondue dish). Cover. Let rise in warm place until doubled in size. Bake in 350° F oven 40 minutes, or until golden brown and loaf sounds hollow when thumped. Cool 10 minutes. Remove from pan. Makes 1 round loaf.

TURKISH CHEESE BREAD

This open-face cheese bread is shaped like an elongated pizza. Serve it hot, sliced in narrow strips for an appetizer or in wider chunks for luncheon.

1 pkg. active dry yeast
1/4 cup warm water
6 tbs. soft butter
2 tbs. sugar
3 eggs
1/2 tsp. salt
1/2 cup lukewarm milk
3-1/4 cups all-purpose flour
Cheese Filling

Sprinkle yeast into warm water and let stand until dissolved. Beat butter and sugar until creamy. Beat in eggs, one at a time. Add salt, milk, dissolved yeast and 1 cup flour. Beat until smooth. Gradually add enough flour to make a soft dough. Turn out on a floured board and knead until smooth. Place in a greased bowl. Cover with a clean kitchen towel and let rise untll doubled, about 1-1/2 hours. Turn out on a floured board and knead lightly. Cut into 8 pieces. Roll each into a thin rectangle, about 5 x 9-inches. Place on greased baking sheets. Spread with Cheese Filling. Roll up edges slightly to hold in filling. Let rise 20 minutes. Bake in a 375° F oven 25 minutes or until golden brown. Makes 8 cheese breads.

Cheese Filling: Beat together 1/2 pound <u>each</u> cream cheese and ricotta cheese, 2/3 cup grated Parmesan cheese, 3 eggs, 1/4 cup chopped parsley and 3 green onions, chopped. Use as directed.

FINNISH CELEBRATION BREAD

This fruit and nut filled sweet bread is traditionally baked in a milking pail to celebrate the birth of spring calves.

2 pkg. active dry yeast
1/2 cup warm water
3/4 cup <u>each</u> butter and sugar
4 eggs
1 tsp. salt
1/2 tsp. nutmeg
2 tsp. grated lemon peel
1-3/4 cups lukewarm milk
7 to 8 cups all-purpose flour
3/4 cup chopped filberts <u>or</u> walnuts

62

Stir yeast into water. Let stand until dissolved. Cream butter and sugar. Beat in eggs, salt, nutmeg, lemon peel and milk. Stir in dissolved yeast.

Gradually add 4 cups flour. Beat well for 5 minutes. Gradually beat in enough remaining flour to make a soft dough. Turn out on a floured board and knead until smooth and satiny. Place in a greased bowl. Butter top of dough lightly. Cover and let rise in a warm place until almost doubled in size. Turn out on a floured board and knead lightly. Shape into a round ball. Place in a greased 4 quart baking dish. Butter top of dough lightly. Cover and let rise in a warm place until almost doubled. Bake in a 350° F oven 1 hour or until golden brown and bread sounds hollow when thumped. Let cool on a wire cake rack, then turn out of pan. Makes 1 large loaf.

SWISS CINNAMON BRAID

This spicy-sweet bread is ideal for breakfast or a coffee treat.

1 pkg. active dry yeast
1/4 cup warm water
1/2 cup milk
1/4 cup butter
2 tbs. sugar
1 tsp. salt
2 eggs
3 cups all-purpose flour
Cinnamon-Sugar: 1/4 cup sugar blended with 1-1/2 tsp. cinnamon

64

Sprinkle yeast into warm water. Stir until dissolved. Heat milk and butter until butter melts. Pour into a large mixing bowl. Add sugar and salt. Cool to lukewarm. Stir in yeast mixture. Beat in eggs, one at a time. Gradually beat in enough flour to make a soft dough. Turn out on a floured board. Knead until smooth and satiny. Place in a greased bowl. Butter top of dough lightly. Cover with kitchen towel. Let rise in a warm place until doubled, about 1-1/2 hours. Turn out on floured board. Knead lightly. Cut into 3 pieces. Roll each piece between the palms of your hands, making strips about 10 inches long. Roll strips in Cinnamon-Sugar. Place sugared strips on a buttered baking sheet and braid. Tuck ends under braid. Cover. Let rise in warm place until doubled in size. Bake in 350° F oven 30 to 35 minutes, or until golden brown. Cool on cake rack. Makes 1 large braid.

65

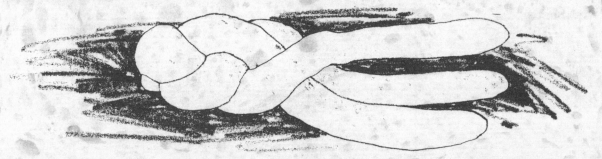

Specialty Rolls

67

HOLLAND BRIOCHE CAKES

These aromatic lemon buns are delightful for brunch. If you intend to freeze some, wait and frost those later.

1 pkg. active dry yeast
1/4 cup warm water
3/4 cup milk
1/3 cup sugar
1/3 cup butter
1 tsp. salt
2 eggs
1 tsp. grated lemon peel
1 tbs. lemon juice
3-1/2 cups all-purpose flour
melted butter

Sprinkle yeast into warm water. Let stand until dissolved. Heat milk. Pour over sugar, butter and salt in large mixing bowl. Let cool to lukewarm. Add dissolved yeast, eggs, lemon peel and juice. Beat until smooth. Gradually add half of the flour. Beat 2 minutes. Stir in remaining flour. Beat well. Turn out on floured board. Knead until smooth and satiny. Place in a greased bowl. Cover with a kitchen towel. Let rise until doubled in size, about 1-1/2 hours. Turn out on floured board. Knead lightly. Roll out to about 1/4 inch in thickness. Brush with melted butter. Fold over in thirds. The total width of the dough should be 9 inches. With a sharp knife, cut into 1/2 inch strips. Twist, form a loop, and tuck ends underneath. Place on greased baking sheets. Cover. Let rise until doubled. Bake in 375° F oven 15 to 20 minutes, or until golden brown. Cool on a rack. Spread with Orange Frosting. Makes 2 dozen.

Orange Frosting: Blend 1 cup powdered sugar with 1 tablespoon orange juice.

HOT CROSS BUNS

Spicy hot cross buns have been an English tradition for centuries. Originally they were passed out to holiday journeyers.

1 pkg. active dry yeast	1 cup milk
4 cups all-purpose flour	1/4 cup butter
1/3 cup sugar	2 eggs
1/2 tsp. salt	1/2 cup currants
3/4 tsp. cinnamon	1/4 cup diced citron (optional)
1/4 tsp. nutmeg	Lemon Glaze

Combine yeast, 1 cup flour, sugar, salt, cinnamon and nutmeg in a mixing bowl. Heat milk and butter to about 125°. Pour over dry ingredients and beat until smooth. Beat in eggs, one at a time. Gradually add remaining flour, beating with a heavy duty electric mixer or wooden spoon. Mix in currants and citron. Turn out on a floured board and knead until smooth and satiny. Place in a greased bowl and butter top lightly. Cover, and let rise in a warm place until almost doubled in size. Turn dough out on a floured board and knead lightly. Cut off pieces about the size of a golf ball. Roll between the palms of your hands. Place on a lightly greased baking sheet. Cover and let rise until almost doubled in size. With a razor blade or sharp knife, cut a cross in the surface of each bun. Bake in a 375° F oven 15 to 20 minutes, or until golden brown. Let cool on a cake rack.

Lemon Glaze: Blend together 1 cup powdered sugar, 1 teaspoon grated lemon peel and 1-1/2 tablespoons milk. Drizzle over tops of buns in a cross design. Makes about 2 dozen.

71

LEBANESE ANISE BUNS (Ka'ick)

1 pkg. active dry yeast
3 cups all-purpose flour
1/2 cup sugar
1 tsp. anise seed
1/2 tsp. salt

3/4 cup milk
1/2 cup butter
1 egg
Orange Flower Syrup

Combine yeast, 1 cup flour, sugar, anise seed and salt in a mixing bowl. Heat milk and butter to about 125°. Pour over the dry ingredients and beat until smooth. Beat in egg. Gradually add enough remaining flour to make a soft dough. Turn out on a lightly floured board and knead until smooth and satiny. Place in a greased bowl. Butter top of dough lightly. Cover and let rise in a warm place until almost doubled in size. Turn dough out on a floured board and knead lightly. Cut into small pieces, about 2 inches in diameter. Cover with a towel and let rest 10 minutes. On a lightly floured board, roll into discs about 3-1/2 inches in diameter and 1/4 inch thick. Place on lightly greased baking sheet. Let rise in a warm place until almost doubled. Bake in a

350° F oven 15 to 20 minutes, or until golden brown. Let cool on wire racks. Using a fork, dip breads one at a time into the hot syrup, coating completely. Place on a serving tray to cool. Makes about 2 dozen.

Orange Flower Syrup: Combine 1/2 cup sugar, 1/4 cup milk, 2 tablespoons butter and 1 teaspoon orange flower water or rose water in a saucepan. Bring to a boil and boil 2 minutes. Use as directed.

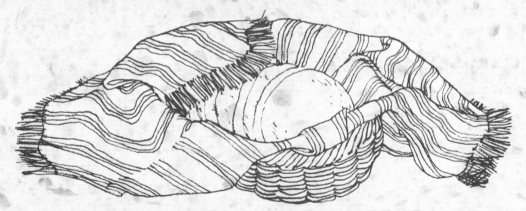

73

CARAMEL CINNAMON TWISTS

Caramelized cinnamon-sugar gilds these spiral rolls with crunchy candy.

1 cup butter, melted
1 cup sour cream
1 tsp. salt
1 tsp. vanilla
1 pkg. active dry yeast
2 egg yolks
1 egg
3-1/2 cups all-purpose flour
1-1/2 cups sugar
2 tsp. cinnamon

74

Mix together hot butter, sour cream, salt and vanilla. The mixture should be lukewarm. Sprinkle in yeast. Beat egg yolks and egg until blended. Stir into yeast mixture. Stir in enough flour to make a soft dough. Beat until smooth. It is not necessary to knead this dough. Cover bowl with plastic wrap. Chill 2 hours. Mix sugar and cinnamon. Spread half of it on a board. Divide dough in half. Roll each piece of dough into a rectangle (15 x 18 inches). Turn dough in the cinnamon-sugar mixture so both sides are coated. Fold over three times, as you would fold a letter. Repeat rolling, coating and folding three times until sugar mixture is almost used. Roll into a rectangle 1/4 inch thick. Cut into strips 1/2 inch wide by 4 inches long. Twist strips. Dip in remaining cinnamon-sugar mixture. Lay on a greased baking sheet. Repeat with remaining dough and sugar mixture. Cover with towel. Let rise in a warm place until light and puffy. Bake in 375° F oven 15 minutes, or until golden brown. Serve hot or reheat. Makes about 4 dozen twists.

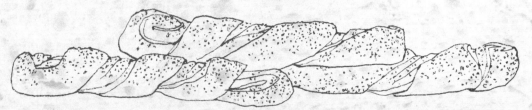

FILBERT CRESCENTS

A delectable filbert paste swirls within these tender refrigerator crescents.

1 pkg. active dry yeast
1/4 cup warm water
1/2 cup butter
3 cups all-purpose flour
1/3 cup light cream or milk
1/4 cup sugar
1/2 tsp. ground cardamom
3 eggs
Nut Filling
1 egg white
1/2 cup chopped filberts
sugar

Sprinkle yeast into warm water. Let stand until dissolved. Cut butter into flour until mixture resembles oatmeal. Heat cream or milk until lukewarm. Pour into a large mixing bowl. Add sugar and cardamom. Stir in dissolved yeast and 1 cup butter-flour mixture. Beat until smooth. Beat in eggs, one at a time. Add remaining butter-flour mixture. Beat until smooth. (It is not necessary to knead this dough.) Cover with plastic wrap or foil. Chill several hours or overnight. Divide chilled dough into four equal pieces. Roll out each piece on a lightly floured board, into a circle about 15 inches in diameter. Spread 1/4 of the nut filling over each circle of dough. Cut each circle into 8 pie-shaped wedges. Roll wedges up starting at large end. Place on greased baking sheets with the points underneath. Curve rolls to form crescents. Cover with a towel. Let rise in a warm place until doubled. Beat egg white lightly. Brush over top of crescents. Sprinkle with filberts and sugar. Bake in 350°F oven 20 minutes, or until golden brown. Makes 32 rolls.

Nut Filling: Combine 1 cup filberts or blanched almonds, 1/2 cup sugar and 1 egg in blender container. Cover. Blend until smooth. Stir mixture into 1/3 cup soft butter. Use as directed.

CARAMEL PECAN ROLLS

Children adore these wonderful chewy, sticky rolls.

2 pkg. active dry yeast
1/2 cup warm water
1 cup milk
1/2 cup butter
2/3 cup sugar
1 tsp. salt
1 tsp. vanilla

3 eggs
5 cups all-purpose flour
melted butter
cinnamon
1 cup light brown sugar
Caramel Pecan Coating

Sprinkle yeast into warm water. Let stand until dissolved. Heat milk and butter together until butter melts. Pour into a large mixing bowl. Stir in sugar, salt and vanilla. Cool to lukewarm. Stir in yeast mixture. Add eggs one at a time. Beat until smooth. Gradually beat in enough flour to make a soft dough. Turn out on a floured board. Knead until smooth and satiny. Place in a greased bowl. Butter top of dough lightly. Cover with kitchen towel. Let rise until doubled in size, about 1-1/2 hours. Divide dough in half and knead lightly. Roll each piece into a 10 x 12-inch rectangle. Spread with melted butter. Sprinkle lightly with cinnamon. Scatter 1/2 cup brown sugar onto each rectangle. Roll up. Cut into 3/4 inch slices. Place in prepared caramel-coated pans. Cover. Let rise until doubled in size. Bake in 350° F oven 30 minutes, or until golden brown. Immediately turn upside down on racks and lift off pans. Serve warm or cool. Makes about 3 dozen rolls.

Caramel Pecan Coating: Select three 9-inch square baking pans. Place 2-1/2 tablespoons butter, 1/4 cup light corn syrup, and 2/3 cup firmly packed light brown sugar in each pan. Heat in 350° F oven just until butter melts and mixture bubbles. Spread coating evenly over bottom of pans. Scatter 1/3 cup pecan halves onto each caramel coated pan. Top with cinnamon slices as directed.

FROSTED PINWHEELS

Orange frosting glazes raisin-studded pinwheels.

2 pkg. active dry yeast
1/2 cup warm water
1 cup milk
3/4 cup butter
1/3 cup sugar
1/2 tsp. salt

1/2 tsp. almond extract
6 eggs
6-1/2 cups all-purpose flour
Raisin Filling
Orange Frosting

80   Sprinkle yeast into warm water. Let stand until dissolved. Heat milk to lukewarm. Cream butter and sugar. Beat in salt, extract and eggs. Stir in dissolved yeast and milk. Gradually add enough flour to make a soft dough. Turn out onto floured board and knead until smooth and satiny. Place in greased bowl. Cover with a kitchen towel and let rise in warm place until doubled. Punch down. Turn out onto floured board and knead lightly. Roll out into a large rectangle about 1/3 inch thick. Spread with Raisin Filling. Roll up

and cut into 1/2 inch thick slices. Place on greased baking sheets 2 inches apart. Cover and let rise in a warm place until doubled, about 45 minutes. Bake in 375° F oven 20 to 25 minutes or until golden brown. Cool slightly. Spread with Orange Frosting. Makes about 3 dozen.

Raisin Filling: Mix together 3/4 cup brown sugar, 1/2 cup raisins, 3 tablespoons melted butter and 1 tablespoon cinnamon. Use as directed.

Orange Frosting: Mix together 2 cups powdered sugar and 2 tablespoons each orange juice concentrate and water. Use as directed.

CINNAMON ROLLS 81

Follow directions for Frosted Pinwheels except place 12 slices in each of three greased 9 x 1-1/2-inch round cake pans. Cover and let rise in a warm place until doubled in size, about 30 minutes. Bake in 375° F oven about 20 to 25 minutes. Drizzle vanilla or Orange Frosting over warm rolls.

DANISH PASTRY COCKSCOMBS

Here are Bear Claws, an all-time favorite.

1 pkg. active dry yeast
1/2 cup lukewarm water
5 cups all-purpose flour
1-1/2 cups butter
2 eggs
1 egg, separated
1 cup milk, heated to lukewarm

3 tbs. sugar
1 tsp. salt
1 tsp. ground cardamom
Almond Cream Filling
1 egg white lightly beaten
coarse granulated sugar

82

Sprinkle yeast into lukewarm water and let stand until dissolved. Measure 4 cups flour into a mixing bowl. Cut in 1/2 cup butter until the size of peas. Add eggs, egg yolk, milk, yeast, sugar, salt and cardamom. Mix until blended. Gradually stir in remaining flour. Turn dough out onto a floured board and knead until light. Roll into a rectangle 1/2 inch thick, 12 inches wide and 18 inches long. Cut remaining butter into thin slices. Place half of it on the center strip of the rectangle. Fold over 1 side. Place remaining butter on top and fold over remaining side. Roll out 1/2 inch thick and fold in thirds. Place on a baking pan and cover with plastic wrap. Chill 15 minutes. Repeat rolling and folding 3 times. Dough is then ready for shaping. Roll out into a long strip. Cut in 6 strips, each 3 to 4 inches wide. Roll each strip 1/8 inch thick, 5 inches wide and 21 inches long. Mark off into thirds, lengthwise. Spread a band of filling down the center third. Fold one side of dough over the center. Fold remaining third on top. Flip over, seam side down, and cut crosswise in 3 inch wide pieces. Make 3 deep gashes in each piece along one folded edge. Place on buttered baking sheet and let rise until doubled, about 1 hour. Brush with slightly beaten egg white and sprinkle with sugar. Bake in 375° F oven 15 to 20 minutes, or until golden brown. Makes 3 dozen.

Almond Cream Filling: Beat together 1/4 cup butter, 1 cup powdered sugar, 2 egg yolks, 2 tablespoons rum and 1 cup ground almonds. Use as directed.

DINNER ROLLS

2 pkg. active dry yeast
1/2 cup warm water
1 cup milk
1/2 cup butter
2 tbs. sugar

1 tsp. salt
1 tsp. vanilla or grated lemon peel
3 eggs
5 cups all-purpose flour
1 egg white, lightly beaten

84

Sprinkle yeast into warm water. Let stand until dissolved. Heat milk and butter together until butter melts. Pour into large mixing bowl. Stir in sugar, salt and vanilla or lemon peel. Cool to lukewarm. Stir in dissolved yeast. Add eggs one at a time. Beat until smooth. Gradually beat in enough flour to make a soft dough. Turn out on a floured board. Knead until smooth and satiny. Place in a greased bowl. Butter top of dough lightly. Cover and let rise in a warm place until doubled in size, about 1-1/2 hours. Punch down. Turn out onto floured board. Shape in any of the following ways. Cover with towel. Let rise until doubled. Bake in 375° F oven 15 minutes or until golden brown. Makes 3 to 5 dozen rolls, depending on style.

SHAPING DINNER ROLLS

Bowknots: Roll dough about 1/2 inch thick. Cut into 9-inch long strips. Tie in loose knots. Tuck ends under. Place on greased baking sheets. Cover. Let rise in warm place. Bake as directed.

Cloverleaf Rolls: Shape dough into small balls about 3/4 inch in diameter. Place 3 balls in each greased muffin cup. Cover. Let rise in warm place until doubled. Bake as directed.

Crescents: Roll dough into 12-inch circles about 1/4 inch thick. Brush with melted butter. Cut into 8 to 12 wedges. Starting at the wide side, roll up. Shape rolls into crescents. Place on a greased baking sheet. Let rise until doubled in size. Bake as directed.

Parker House Rolls: Roll dough 1/2 inch thick. Cut with a 3 to 4 inch round cutter. Brush with melted butter. Fold in half. Press edges to seal. Place on greased baking sheet. Cover. Let rise until doubled. Bake as directed.

86

Rosettes: Roll dough about 1/2 inch thick and cut into 12 inch strips. Form into a loose knot, leaving two long ends. Tuck top end under roll. Bring bottom end up and tuck into center of roll. Place on greased baking sheets. Cover. Let rise until doubled. Bake as directed.

Corkscrews: Roll dough about 1/2 inch thick. Cut into 8 inch long strand. Wrap each one around a greased wooden clothespin. Seal ends. Place on greased baking sheets. Cover. Let rise until doubled. Bake as directed. Remove clothespins after baking.

Braids: Form dough into several ropes about 1/2 inch in diameter. Braid 3 ropes at a time into a long braid. Cut into 3-1/2 inch lengths. Pinch together at each end. Pull braid slightly to lengthen it. Place on greased baking sheets. Cover. Let rise until doubled. Bake as directed.

87

CROISSANTS

Flakiness is achieved by cutting butter into the flour as when making pastry. Butter nuggets melt as the rolls bake making many paper-thin layers.

1 pkg. active dry yeast
1/4 cup warm water
2 egg yolks
1 cup lukewarm milk
1 tbs. sugar
1/2 tsp. salt
3-1/3 cups all-purpose flour
1 cup butter
1 egg white, beaten until frothy

Sprinkle yeast into warm water and let stand until dissolved. Beat egg yolks. Stir in warm milk, sugar, salt, yeast mixture and 2/3 cup flour. Beat until smooth and set aside. In another bowl, cut butter into remaining flour until particles are the size of large peas. Pour in yeast mixture. Mix lightly with a spatula just until flour is moistened. Cover bowl with plastic wrap or foil. Chill at least 2 hours or until cold. (If desired, chill up to 3 days). Turn out onto floured board and knead lightly. Divide into thirds. Roll each piece of dough into a circle about 16 inches in diameter. Cut into 12 pie-shaped wedges. For each croissant, roll wedges starting at the outer edge of the circle. Place rolls point down on a greased baking sheet. Cover with a towel and let rise at room temperature until doubled. Brush surface with beaten egg white. Bake in 375° F oven 20 minutes or until golden brown. Serve warm. Makes 3 dozen rolls.

FRENCH-STYLE CRUSTY ROLLS

A remarkably crisp crust distinguishes these round white buns. They freeze and reheat beautifully, retaining their crunch.

1 pkg. active dry yeast
1-1/2 cups warm water
3-1/4 cups all-purpose flour
1-1/2 tsp. salt
cornmeal
Egg White Glaze: 1 egg white lightly beaten with 1 tsp. water

90

Sprinkle yeast into warm water in a large mixing bowl. Let stand until dissolved. Gradually add flour, beating until smooth. Turn dough out onto a lightly floured board and knead until smooth and satiny. Place in a greased bowl and butter top of dough lightly. Cover with a clean kitchen towel and let rise in a warm place until doubled in size, about 1-1/2 hours. Punch down, cover with a towel and let rise again until doubled in size. Turn out onto a

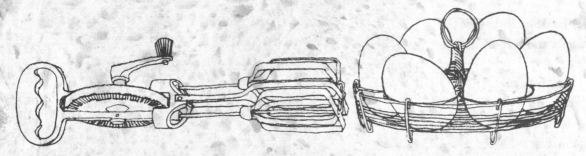

floured board and knead lightly. Cut into 18 equal pieces. Shape each piece into a round ball. Place on a greased baking sheet that is lightly sprinkled with cornmeal. Brush with Egg White Glaze. Place in a warm place to rise (not in the oven). Make a tent with a tightly wrung out, wet kitchen towel to cover the rolls while they are rising. This is important as it helps make the crust crispy. To prepare the oven for baking the rolls, place a pan of hot water on the lower rack and preheat to 375° F. When rolls have doubled in size, brush again with glaze and bake on the rack above the steaming water 15 minutes. Brush again with glaze and bake 15 minutes longer, or until golden brown. Makes 18 rolls.

PITA (Arabic, Mediterranean, or Pocket Bread)

Various names identify this fun, saucer-like bread. Each round puffs up like a balloon during baking, then collapses forming a neat inner pocket.

2 cups warm water
1 pkg. active dry yeast
2 tsp. sugar
4-1/2 cups all-purpose flour
1-1/2 tsp. salt
3 tbs. olive oil or vegetable oil

Place 1/4 cup water in a small bowl. Add yeast and sugar. Stir just to blend. Let stand until dissolved. Place flour, salt, and oil in a mixing bowl. Add yeast mixture and remaining 1-3/4 cups water. Beat with a heavy duty electric mixer or wooden spoon until flour is completely moistened. Turn dough out onto a lightly floured board and knead until smooth and no longer sticky, about 5 or 10 minutes. Place in a greased bowl and oil top of dough lightly. Cover with a clean kitchen towel and let rise in a warm place until doubled in size, about 1-1/4 hours. Turn out on floured board and knead lightly to remove air bubbles. Roll into a log 12 inches long. Cut into 12 equal pieces. Pat each piece of dough into a ball. Using a rolling pin, roll each ball of dough on a floured board into a 6-1/2-inch round, about 1/4 inch thick. Place on lightly greased baking sheets. Let rise in a warm place, uncovered, until barely doubled in thickness. Move oven rack to lowest slot and preheat oven to 500° F. Bake 1 pan at a time about 5 minutes, or until puffed and just starting to brown. Remove from oven and place on cake racks. Serve while warm or let cool slightly and slip into plastic bags to stay moist and pliable. If desired, freeze. To serve later, let thaw, stack together and wrap in foil. Reheat in 375° F oven 10 to 15 minutes, or until hot through. Makes 12 pitas.

ITALIAN SALT STICKS

3 cups all-purpose flour
1 tbs. sugar
1 tsp. salt
1 pkg. active dry yeast
1/4 cup olive oil _or_ salad oil

1-1/4 cups very warm water (125°)
Glaze: 1 egg white lightly beaten
     with 1 tbs. water
coarse salt

94

Place 1 cup flour, sugar, salt and yeast in the large bowl of an electric mixer. Add oil. Gradually stir in water. Beat at medium speed 2 minutes. Add 1/2 cup flour. Beat at high speed 2 minutes. Using a heavy duty mixer or wooden spoon, add enough remaining flour to make a soft dough. Turn out onto a well floured board. Knead several minutes. Work dough into a smooth ball. Shape into a log. Cut into 20 equal-sized pieces. Roll each piece into a rope about 16 inches long. Or, make small ropes 6 to 8 inches long. Arrange 1 inch apart on oiled baking sheets. Roll to spread oil on all sides. Cover. Let rise in a warm place until puffy, about 15 minutes. Paint each stick with Glaze. Sprinkle with coarse salt. Bake in 325° F oven 25 to 30 minutes or until browned. Makes 20 16-inch bread sticks.

ONION BUNS

These robust whole wheat buns are excellent with hamburgers.

3 tbs. butter
1 cup finely chopped onion
3 cups <u>each</u> all-purpose and whole wheat flour
3 tbs. sugar
2 tsp. salt
2 pkg. active dry yeast
2 cups very warm water (125° F)

Melt butter in frying pan. Saute onion until golden, about 5 to 7 minutes. Set aside. Blend together 1 cup all-purpose flour, 1 cup whole wheat flour, sugar, salt and yeast in large electric mixer bowl. Reserve 2 tablespoons of the onion-butter mixture. Add remainder to dry ingredients. Pour in warm water. Beat at low speed 2 minutes. Add 1 cup whole wheat flour. Beat at high speed 2 minutes. Stir in remaining 1 cup whole wheat flour and enough of the all-purpose flour (about 1 cup) to make a soft dough. Sprinkle about 1/3 cup all-purpose flour on bread board. Turn dough out onto it and knead until smooth and elastic, about 5 minutes. Add more flour as needed. Place in a greased bowl and butter top of dough lightly. Cover and let rise in a warm place until doubled in size. Punch dough down and divide into 36 golf ball-size pieces. Shape into buns. Place 1/2 inch apart on greased baking sheets. Sprinkle 1/4 teaspoon reserved onion on the top of each bun. Cover with a towel and let rise in a warm place until doubled in size. Bake in a 375° F oven 20 to 25 minutes or until golden brown. Makes 36 rolls.

97

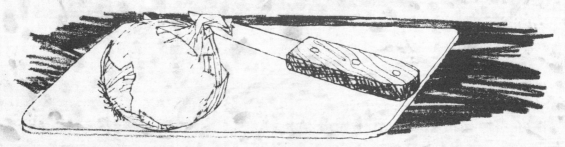

SESAME HAMBURGER BUNS

Plump, freshly-made hamburger buns are always a big hit at a barbecue. Split and toast them on the grill, if you like.

1 pkg. active dry yeast
1/4 cup warm water
1/2 cup butter
2 tbs. sugar
3 eggs
1 cup milk (room temp.)
1 tsp. salt
4 cups all-purpose flour
1 egg white lightly beaten
1/4 cup sesame seeds

Sprinkle yeast into warm water and let stand until dissolved. Cream butter and sugar. Beat in eggs, milk and salt. Add dissolved yeast. Gradually add enough flour to make a soft dough. Turn out onto a lightly floured board and knead until smooth and satiny. Place dough in a greased bowl and butter top lightly. Cover with a clean kitchen towel. Let rise in a warm place until doubled in size. Punch dough down. Turn out onto a floured board and knead lightly. Divide into 24 balls. Turn each ball in hands, folding edges under to make an even circle. Press flat between hands. Place on greased baking sheets. Press to 3-1/4 inch circle. Cover with towel and let rise in a warm place until doubled in size. Brush with lightly beaten egg white and sprinkle with sesame seeds. Bake in 375° F oven 10 to 15 minutes or until golden brown. Cool on cake rack or serve warm. Makes 2 dozen buns.

MEXICAN PAN DULCE

Top these fanciful Mexican sweet buns with either plain or chocolate strusel and shape them in any of several different ways.

1 cup milk
1/3 cup butter
1 pkg. active dry yeast
1 tsp. salt
1/3 cup sugar
3-1/4 cups all-purpose flour
100 2 eggs
Plain Streusel
Chocolate Streusel
Egg wash: 1 egg beaten with 2 tbs. milk

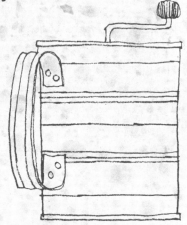

Place milk and butter in saucepan and heat until very warm, about 125°. Place yeast, salt, sugar, and 1 cup flour in a large mixing bowl. Pour in heated milk mixture and beat until smoothly blended. Add eggs, one at a time, and beat until smooth. Gradually add remaining flour and beat until smooth. Turn out onto a floured board and knead 10 minutes, or until satiny and no longer sticky. Place in a greased bowl. Butter top of dough lightly. Cover with a clean kitchen towel and let rise in a warm place until doubled in size. Turn out on a floured board and knead lightly. Cut dough into 14 equal pieces and shape each into a ball. Then finish in a variety of ways, following the directions given on pages 102 and 103. Complete with streusel, using Plain Streusel on half of the buns and Chocolate Streusel on the other. Place on a lightly greased baking sheet and let rise until doubled in size, about 45 minutes. Brush lightly with egg wash. Bake in 375° F oven 20 minutes, or until golden brown. Makes 14 various shaped buns.

101

Plain Streusel: In a bowl blend 3/4 cup sugar, 1 cup flour and 6 tablespoons butter until crumbly. Blend in 3 egg yolks. Makes enough for 7 buns.

Chocolate Streusel: Prepare Plain Streusel, adding 1/4 cup unsweetened cocoa to dry ingredients. Use for remaining 7 buns.

Concho (shell): For each bun, shape dough ball into a 3 inch round, 3/4 inch thick, and place on a greased baking sheet. Take 1/4 cup plain or chocolate streusel and pat into a ball. Then on a lightly floured board, roll into a 3-inch round, 1/8 inch thick. Lay streusel on dough, pressing in lightly. With a small sharp knife, score streusel in 4 or 5 arcs to resemble a shell. Or for square-topped style, score streusel in straight lines 3/8 inch apart, and score again in lines 3/8 inch apart, making small squares. Bake as directed.

Picon (coffeecake): Shape dough balls as for Concho. Sprinkle streusel on top of dough, piling it about 1/2 inch thick. Pat it over the entire surface. Bake as directed.

102

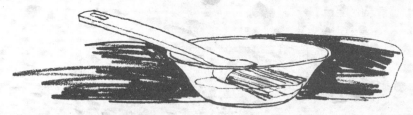

Elote (corn): On a lightly floured surface, roll out each ball of dough about 4 inches wide and 8 inches long. Sprinkle entire surface with 2 tablespoons streusel. Roll up, pulling the ends slightly to stretch them. Place on a greased baking sheet and score surface with crosswise slashes 1/4 inch apart. Bake as directed.

Cuerno mantequilla (butterhorn): On a floured surface, roll out each ball of dough about 4 inches wide and 8 inches long. Sprinkle entire surface with 2 tablespoons streusel. Roll in the long sides tapering to a point. Take the long end and pulling it gently, roll up making a crescent. Place on a greased baking sheet. Bake as directed.

103

International Holiday Breads

PANETONNE

Chewy raisins and nuts jewel this sweet brioche-style Italian bread.

3/4 cup milk
1 pkg. active dry yeast
1/4 cup lukewarm water
1/2 cup butter
1/2 cup sugar
3 eggs
3-1/2 cups all-purpose flour
1 tsp. <u>each</u> vanilla and grated lemon peel
1/2 tsp. cinnamon
1/2 cup each golden and dark raisins, plumped in brandy <u>or</u> dry sherry
1/2 cup slivered almonds <u>or</u> pine nuts
1 egg white, lightly beaten

Heat milk until warm. Sprinkle yeast into warm water and let stand until dissolved. Beat butter until creamy. Beat in sugar. Add eggs one at a time. Beat until smooth. Add 1 cup flour. Beat well. Stir in yeast, milk, vanilla, lemon peel and cinnamon. Gradually add remaining flour. Beat until smooth. Mix in raisins and almonds. Turn out on a lightly floured board and knead until smooth and no longer sticky. Place in a greased bowl. Butter top of dough lightly. Cover with a clean kitchen towel and let rise in a warm place until doubled in size. Turn out onto a floured board and knead lightly. Divide in half. Shape into two round cakes about 6 inches in diameter. Place on a greased baking sheet or in greased cake pans. Cover and let rise until doubled in size. Bake in 350° F oven 30 minutes, or until golden brown. Let cool on a cake rack. Slice and serve warm or at room temperature. Makes 2 round loaves.

PORTUGUESE SWEET BREAD

During baking this citrus-scented loaf forms a crackly sugar-crust.

1 pkg. active dry yeast
1/4 cup warm water
1/2 cup milk
1/4 cup butter
1/2 cup sugar
1/2 tsp. salt
2 eggs
2 tsp. grated lemon peel
3-1/2 cups all-purpose flour
Egg Glaze: 1 egg yolk beaten with I tbs. milk

Sprinkle yeast into warm water and let stand until dissolved. Heat milk and butter until butter melts. Pour into a mixing bowl containing sugar and salt and let cool to lukewarm. Add eggs one at a time. Stir in lemon peel and yeast

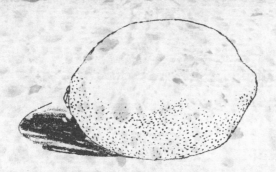

mixture. Gradually beat in flour, adding enough to make a soft dough. Turn out on a lightly floured board and knead until smooth and satiny. Place in a greased bowl. Butter top of dough lightly. Cover with a kitchen towel and let rise in a warm place until doubled in size. Turn out on a lightly floured board and knead gently. Shape into a flat cake about 9 inches in diameter. Place in a greased 9-inch spring form pan, with removable bottom, or on a greased baking sheet. Cover with a towel and let rise in a warm place until doubled in size. Brush with Egg Glaze. Bake in 325°F oven 35 to 40 minutes or until golden brown. Let cool on a cake rack, then remove from pan. Slice and serve warm with sweet butter. Makes 1 large loaf.

KULICH

This Russian Easter bread bakes in a two-pound coffee can to achieve its stately height. It is traditional to lay a single rosebud on top of the frosting glaze.

1 pkg. active dry yeast
2-1/2 cups all-purpose flour
1/4 cup sugar
1/2 tsp. salt
1/2 cup milk
6 tbs. butter
1 egg

2 egg yolks
1 tsp. grated lemon peel
1/4 cup each golden and dark raisins
2 tbs. sherry
1/4 cup chopped blanched almonds
Powdered Sugar Glaze: 1/2 cup powdered sugar blended with 1-1/2 tsp. milk

Combine yeast, 1 cup flour, sugar and salt in a large bowl. Heat milk and butter until very warm (approximately 125°). Pour into dry ingredients and beat until smooth. Beat in egg, egg yolks and lemon peel. Gradually add remaining flour, beating well after each addition. Soak raisins in sherry. Add to dough along with almonds. Turn dough out onto a lightly floured board and knead until smooth and satiny. Place in a greased bowl and butter top of dough lightly. Cover with a clean kitchen towel and let rise in a warm place until doubled in size, about 1-1/2 hours. Turn dough onto a lightly floured board and knead gently a few times. Butter a two-pound coffee can. Fold a doubled sheet of foil around top of can to extend it 2 inches. Shape dough into a ball and place in can. Loosely cover top of can with plastic wrap or foil. Let dough rise in a warm place until doubled in size, or until dough almost reaches the top of the can. Bake in 350° F oven 50 minutes, or until skewer inserted in the center comes out clean and the loaf sounds hollow when thumped. Let cool on a cake rack. Spread frosting over top of dough letting it drizzle down the sides. To serve, cut off the frosted top and place in the center of a board. Cut remaining loaf lengthwise, then in crosswise slices and arrange on board around top. Makes 1 tall loaf.

DANISH COFFEE TWIST

The simple way in which this buttery yeast bread is cut and shaped results in its handsome pinwheel design. You have a choice of three fillings.

1 pkg. active dry yeast
1/4 cup warm water
1/2 cup butter
6 tbs. sugar
1/2 tsp. salt
1/2 tsp. cardamom or 1 tsp. grated orange peel or 2 tsp. vanilla
3 eggs
4 cups all-purpose flour
3/4 cup warm milk
Caramel, Nut or Chocolate Filling, page 114
1 egg white, beaten until frothy
pecan halves, chopped filberts or slivered almonds

Sprinkle yeast into warm water and let stand until dissolved. Beat butter until creamy. Beat in sugar, salt, flavoring and eggs. Add 1 cup flour and beat well. Add warm milk and dissolved yeast. Beat until smooth. Gradually add remaining flour. Beat until smooth using a heavy duty electric mixer or wooden spoon. Turn out onto a floured board and knead lightly. Cut dough in half. Roll one half into a 10 x 14 inch rectangle. Spread with choice of filling. Roll up and place seam side down on a buttered baking sheet. Repeat with remaining dough and filling. Cut through rolls to within 1/2 inch of the bottom at 3/4 inch intervals. Pull and twist each slice to lay flat. Lay them first to one side and then the other. Cover with a towel and let rise in a warm place until doubled in size, about 45 minutes. Brush loaves with egg white and sprinkle with sugar and nuts. Bake in 325° F oven 30 to 35 minutes, or until golden brown. Let cool on cake racks. Serve warm, cut in 1 inch slices.

113

continued

Caramel Pecan Filling: Spread each rectangle with 2 tablespoons butter. Sprinkle each with 1/2 cup firmly packed brown sugar and 1/4 cup chopped pecans. Roll. Proceed as directed.

Nut Streusel Filling: Mix together 1 can (8 oz.) almond paste, 1/4 cup soft butter, 2 tablespoons sugar, 1/3 cup finely chopped filberts, almonds or pecans and 1 egg. Beat until smooth. Spread half of mixture on each rectangle. Roll up. Proceed as directed.

114 **Chocolate Streusel Filling:** Mix 1/2 cup sugar, 1/4 cup all-purpose flour, 2 tablespoons butter, 1-1/2 teaspoons unsweetened ground cocoa and 1/2 teaspoon cinnamon until crumbly. Spread half of mixture on each rectangle. Roll up. Proceed as directed.

DANISH KRINGLER

In Denmark the holiday bread is often pretzel-shaped and delectably filled with almond paste.

6 tbs. soft butter
1-1/2 cups all-purpose flour
1/2 pkg. active dry yeast
2 tbs. warm water
1/4 cup light cream or half-and-half
1 egg

2 tbs. sugar
1/4 tsp. salt
Almond Paste Filling
1 egg white, lightly beaten
granulated sugar for topping
2 tbs. sliced almonds

116

Beat butter and 2 tablespoons flour until blended. With a spatula spread it into a 4 x 8 inch rectangle on a sheet of waxed paper and chill. Sprinkle yeast into warm water in a large mixing bowl and let stand until dissolved. Heat cream just until warm and add to yeast. Mix in egg, sugar and salt. Beat until smooth. Gradually add remaining flour and beat until smooth. Turn out on lightly floured board and knead until smooth and satiny. Roll out into an

8-inch square. Place the chilled butter mixture in the center of dough. Remove paper. Fold dough over chilled mixture from both sides, then fold in thirds. Roll out into a 6 x 12-inch rectangle. Repeat folding and rolling twice more. Wrap in waxed paper and chill 30 minutes. Roll into a 6 x 24-inch rectangle. Spread Almond Paste Filling down the center of dough. Fold dough from each side to cover it. Place on a lightly greased baking sheet and shape into a pretzel. Flatten lightly with a rolling pin. Cover with a towel and let rise at room temperature until doubled. Brush top with egg white. Sprinkle with sugar and sliced almonds. Bake in 375° F oven 20 to 25 minutes, or until golden brown. Makes 1 coffee bread.

Almond Paste Filling: Beat together 1/2 cup almond paste, 2 tablespoons butter, 1 egg white and 1/4 cup shortbread or sugar cookie crumbs. Use as directed.

DRESDEN STOLLEN

Germany boasts many versions of this holiday bread. Here is a famous one that ages and travels well.

3/4 cup dark raisins
1/3 cup <u>each</u> chopped citron
   and candied orange peel
1/4 cup rum
1 pkg. active dry yeast
1/4 cup warm water
1 cup milk
2/3 cup butter

1/2 cup sugar
1 tsp. <u>each</u> salt and grated lemon peel
1/2 tsp. almond extract
2 eggs
4 to 4-1/2 cups all-purpose flour
1/2 cup chopped blanched almonds
melted butter
granulated and powdered sugar

Place raisins, citron and orange peel in bowl. Add rum and let soak 1 hour. Drain and reserve rum. Sprinkle yeast into warm water and let stand until dissolved. Heat milk and butter until butter melts. Pour into a mixing bowl. Add sugar, salt, lemon peel, drained rum and almond extract. Cool to lukewarm. Beat in eggs and dissolved yeast. Gradually add enough flour to make a soft dough. Dredge fruits in flour. Add with almonds to dough and mix well. Turn out on a lightly floured board and knead until smooth and satiny. Place in a greased bowl and butter top of dough lightly. Cover with a kitchen towel and let rise in a warm place until doubled in size, about 1-1/2 to 2 hours. Turn out onto floured board and knead lightly. Divide in half. Roll each piece into an oval about 3/4 inch thick. Brush with melted butter and sprinkle with granulated sugar. Fold over lengthwise, not quite in half, so edges are within 1/2 inch of meeting. Place on greased baking sheets. Brush with melted butter. Cover with towel and let rise until doubled. Bake in 350° F oven 40 minutes or until loaves sound hollow when thumped. Brush with butter and sprinkle generously with powdered sugar while warm. Makes 2 loaves.

119

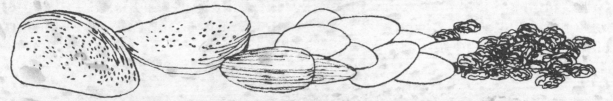

HONEY NUT STOLLEN

Caramelized almonds and honey fill this version of Stollen.

1 pkg. active dry yeast
1/4 cup warm water
1/3 cup sugar
1/2 tsp. salt
1/2 cup warm milk
1/3 cup butter, melted and cooled

2 eggs
1 egg, separated
3-1/4 cups all-purpose flour
Almond Filling
Powdered Sugar Frosting
whole or half nuts for decoration

120   Sprinkle yeast into warm water in a large bowl and let stand until dissolved. Stir in sugar, salt, milk, butter, the whole eggs, and egg yolk. Blend well. Gradually add flour. Beat until smooth. Turn out on lightly floured board and knead until smooth and no longer sticky. Place in a greased bowl and butter top of dough lightly. Cover with a clean kitchen towel and let rise in a warm place until doubled in size, about 1-1/2 to 2 hours. Turn out onto floured

board and knead lightly. Divide in half. Roll each piece into a 9 x 11-inch oval. Place on a greased baking sheet. Mound half of the Almond Filling on one half of the length of one oval. Fold the other half over the filling and pat gently in place. Repeat with remaining filling and dough. Cover with towel. Let rise in a warm place until doubled, about 45 minutes. Brush with lightly beaten egg white. Bake in 325° F oven for 30 to 35 minutes, or until golden brown and loaves sound hollow when thumped. Remove from pans. Let cool on cake rack. When barely warm spread with Powdered Sugar Frosting and decorate with nuts. Serve sliced warm or at room temperature. Makes 2 loaves.

Almond Filling: In a large frying pan heat 1-1/2 tablespoons butter and 1-1/4 cups slivered almonds or chopped pecans. Cook until lightly browned. Cool. Add 2 tablespoons honey or orange marmalade. Use as directed.

Powdered Sugar Frosting: Blend 1 cup unsifted powdered sugar with 1 tablespoon milk and 1 teaspoon vanilla.

GREEK EASTER BREAD (Lambropsomo)

Greeks imbed scarlet eggs in Easter bread using crosses of dough to hold them in place. This bread is named Lambropsomo because it traditionally accompanies roast lamb.

5-1/2 cups all-purpose flour
2/3 cup sugar
1/2 tsp. salt
2 pkg. active dry yeast
1 cup milk
1/2 cup butter
1 tbs. grated lemon peel
1/2 tsp. anise extract (optional)
4 eggs
5 hard-cooked eggs, dyed scarlet

122

Combine 2 cups flour, sugar, salt and yeast in a mixing bowl. Heat milk and butter to about 125°. Pour over dry ingredients and beat until smooth. Add lemon peel, anise extract and eggs, one at a time. Beat well. Gradually add enough remaining flour to make a soft dough. Turn out on a floured board and knead lightly. Place in greased bowl. Cover and let rise until doubled in size. Punch down. Turn out on a floured board and knead lightly. Cut off 1/6 of the dough to use for decoration. Shape remaining dough into a large round loaf, about 10 inches in diameter. Place on a greased baking sheet. Place 1 dyed egg in the center of the dough. Lay the other four around the edge, forming tips of the cross. Roll remaining dough into pencil-thin strips. Place a cross on top of each egg with the strips, pressing the end of the strips into the bread to secure the eggs. Cover and let rise until doubled in size. Brush with slightly beaten egg white. Bake in a 325° F oven 50 to 55 minutes, or until the loaf sounds hollow when thumped. Serve hot or let cool on wire rack. Makes 1 large loaf.

TSOUREKI (Easter Twists)

Another Greek holiday bread is a gala braided crown made with the same dough, and also bedecked with scarlet eggs.

Follow the recipe for Lambropsomo. To shape, divide dough in half. Then divide each half into 3 pieces. Roll into strands, about 24 inches long. Braid 3 strands and form into a wreath. Repeat with remaining 3 strands. Place bread wreaths on greased baking sheets. Arrange 5 hard-cooked eggs, dyed scarlet, in equal spaces around each wreath. Cover and let rise in a warm place until doubled in size. Brush the dough with slightly beaten egg white. Bake in 350° F oven 25 to 30 minutes, or until golden brown. Makes 2 bread twists.

124

ITALIAN EASTER DOVE (Colomba Di Pasqua)

Golden with egg yolks and butter, this sweet bread resembles pound cake.

1 pkg. active dry yeast
1/4 cup warm water
1/2 cup butter
1/2 cup sugar
6 egg yolks
1/2 tsp. salt
3/4 cup warm milk

1 tsp. grated lemon peel
2 tsp. vanilla
4-1/4 cups all-purpose flour
Almond Paste Topping
1 egg white, lightly beaten
granulated sugar
1/4 cup sliced almonds

Sprinkle yeast into warm water. Let stand until dissolved. Beat butter until creamy. Beat in sugar, egg yolks and salt. Stir in warm milk, lemon peel, vanilla and dissolved yeast. Blend in 2 cups flour. Beat 5 minutes. Gradually beat in remaining flour with a heavy duty mixer or wooden spoon. Turn out on a lightly floured board. Knead until smooth. Place in a greased bowl. Butter top of dough lightly. Cover with towel and let rise until doubled in size, about

1-1/2 to 2 hours. Turn dough out onto floured board and knead lightly. Divide into four equal pieces. Roll one piece into an oval, about 4 x 9 inches for the wings. Lay across the width of a large baking sheet. Roll another piece into a triangle about 4 inches wide at the base and 9 inches long. Place like a cross over the wings. Holding the triangle at the center, twist it over once and press the base down for the tail. Pull out a beak with your fingers. With a sharp knife, score the tail to resemble feathers. Repeat each step with remaining dough to make second dove. Spread Almond Paste Topping over wings and tail. Cover and let rise in a warm place until doubled in size. Brush egg white over entire surface of doves. Sprinkle wings and tail with sugar and almonds. Bake in 325° F oven 45 to 50 minutes, or until browned. Makes 2 loaves.

127

 Almond Paste Topping: Beat together 1 egg white, 1/3 cup almond paste and 2 tablespoons sugar. Enough for 2 doves. Use as directed.

Italian Easter Dove pictured on page 125.

BUCCELLATI

Northern Italy contributes this wine-scented, ring-shaped bread.

1 pkg. active dry yeast
1/4 cup warm water
1/2 cup __each__ butter and sugar
4 eggs
1 cup lukewarm milk
2 tsp. anise seed
1 tsp. grated lemon peel
2 tbs. Marsala __or__ Port
1/2 tsp. salt
5 cups all-purpose flour
1 egg white, slightly beaten

Sprinkle yeast into warm water and let stand until dissolved. Cream butter. Beat in sugar and eggs, one at a time. Mix in milk, anise seed, lemon peel,

Marsala and salt. Add 1 cup flour and beat until smooth. Stir in dissolved yeast. Gradually add enough remaining flour to make a soft dough. Turn out on a lightly floured board and knead until smooth and satiny. Place in a greased bowl. Cover, and let rise until doubled in size. Turn out on a lightly floured board and knead a few minutes. Cut into three pieces. Shape each into a round cake. Make a hole in the center of each cake and stretch out making a skinny loop about 8 inches in diameter. Place the rings on a greased baking sheet. Cover, and let rise until doubled in size. Bake in a 375° F oven 25 to 30 minutes or until golden brown. Makes 3 rings.

129

JEWISH CHALLAH

Saffron lends a golden hue to this festive egg bread.

1 pkg. active dry yeast
5 cups all-purpose flour
1 tsp. salt
1/3 cup sugar
1-1/4 cups very warm water (125°)
1/3 cup soft butter or salad oil
2 eggs
pinch of saffron or few drops yellow food coloring
1 egg yolk blended with 1 tbs. milk
1 tbs. sesame seeds

Combine yeast, 1-1/2 cups flour, salt and sugar together in mixing bowl. Stir. Pour in water and beat until smooth. Mix in butter, eggs and saffron or food coloring. Gradually add enough remaining flour to make a soft dough. Turn out on a floured board and knead until dough is smooth and elastic. Place in a greased bowl. Butter top of dough lightly and cover with a clean kitchen towel. Let rise in a warm place until doubled in size, about 1-1/2 hours. Punch dough down. Turn out on a floured board and knead lightly. Divide dough into 4 equal pieces. Roll each to form a strand about 20 inches long. Place the 4 strands lengthwise on a greased baking sheet. Pinch top ends together and braid as follows: Pick up the strand on the right, bring it over the next one, under the third, and over the fourth. Repeat, always starting with strand on right, until braid is complete. Cut enough dough off ends to make 3/4 cup. Tuck ends under and pinch to seal. Roll reserved dough into strip about 18 inches long. Divide into 3 strands and make a small 3 strand braid. Lay on top of large braid. Cover and let rise until doubled. Brush egg yolk mixture evenly over braids and sprinkle with sesame seeds. Bake in 350° F oven 35 minutes, or until loaf sounds hollow when thumped. Makes 1 large braided loaf.

RUSSIAN KRENDL

Sauteed apples, prunes and apricots hide within this pretzel-shaped loaf.

1 pkg. active dry yeast
1/4 cup warm water
1/2 cup milk
1/4 cup butter
2 tbs. sugar
1 tsp. vanilla
1/2 tsp. salt
3 egg yolks

3 cups all-purpose flour
Fruit Filling, page 134
Lemon Frosting, page 134
1 tbs. melted butter
2 tbs. sugar
1/2 tsp. cinnamon
2 tbs. sliced almonds

132

Sprinkle yeast into warm water and let stand until dissolved. Heat milk and butter until lukewarm. Pour over sugar in a mixing bowl. Stir in vanilla, salt, egg yolks and dissolved yeast. Beat until smooth. Gradually add enough flour, beating until smooth after each addition, to make a soft dough. Turn out onto a lightly floured board and knead until smooth. Place in a greased bowl. Butter top of dough lightly and cover with a clean kitchen towel. Let rise in a warm place until doubled in size, about 1-1/2 hours. Meanwhile prepare Fruit Filling and Lemon Frosting. Turn dough out onto floured board and knead lightly. Roll out into a rectangle about 9 inches wide and 28 inches long. Spread with melted butter. Mix sugar and cinnamon. Sprinkle over butter. Spread on Fruit Filling. Roll up starting with the 28-inch side. Pinch edges to seal. Place on a greased baking sheet. Form into a stylized pretzel-shape by bringing one end over the other. Then tuck ends under center of roll. Flatten slightly. Cover with a towel and let rise in a warm place until doubled, about 45 minutes. Bake in 350° F oven 45 minutes, or until golden brown. Let cool slightly. Spread with Lemon Frosting and sprinkle with almonds while loaf is still warm. Makes 1 loaf.

133

continued

Fruit Filling: Peel, core and thinly slice 2 Golden Delicious or Pippin apples. Heat 1 tablespoon butter and 2 tablespoons sugar in a large frying pan. Add apples and cook over medium high heat until just tender. Add 1/3 cup each chopped pitted prunes and dried apricots. Use as directed.

Lemon Frosting: Beat together 2 teaspoons melted butter, 1 teaspoon lemon juice and 3/4 cup powdered sugar. Add a few drop hot water if necessary to thin to a smooth, runny consistency. Use as directed.

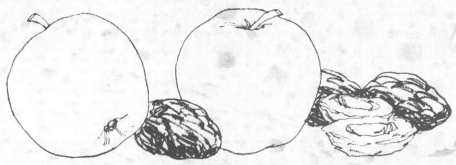

GREEK CHRISTMAS BREAD (Christopsomo)

Look for masticha in a Middle Eastern grocery store.

2 pkg. active dry yeast
1/2 cup warm water
1 cup butter
3/4 cup sugar
4 eggs
1 egg, separated
1/2 cup milk

1/2 cup masticha, pulverized or
   2 tsp. crushed anise seed
1 tsp. salt
5-1/2 cups all-purpose flour
3/4 cup chopped walnuts or pecans (optional)
9 walnut or pecan halves

Sprinkle yeast into warm water and let stand until dissolved. Beat butter until creamy. Blend in sugar, eggs and egg yolk. Heat milk with masticha or anise seed until lukewarm. Add to creamed mixture along with salt. Gradually add half of the flour. Beat hard 5 minutes. Gradually add remaining flour using a heavy duty electric mixer or wooden spoon. Mix in chopped nuts, if desired. Turn dough out onto a lightly floured board and knead until smooth and satiny, about 10 minutes. Place dough in a greased bowl. Butter top lightly and cover with a clean kitchen towel. Let rise in a warm place until doubled in size, about 1-1/2 hours. Turn dough out onto a floured board and knead lightly. Pinch off 2 pieces of dough, each about 3 inches in diameter. Set aside. Shape remaining ball of dough into a smooth flat cake, about 9 inches in diameter. Place on a greased baking sheet. Roll each of the small balls into a 14 inch rope. Cut a 5 inch slash in the end of each. Cross ropes on the center of the round loaf. Curl slashed sections away from center, forming a small circle. Place a walnut half in each circle and one in the center of the cross. Cover loaf with a towel and let rise in a warm place until doubled in size, about 1 hour. Brush the loaf with slightly beaten egg white. Bake in 350° F oven 45 minutes, or until golden brown and the loaf sounds hollow when thumped. Serve hot or let cool on cake rack. To serve, cut in thirds across the loaf and then cut in 1/2 inch slices. Makes 1 extra large loaf.

137

Greek Christmas Bread pictured on page 135.

VIENNESE EASTER TWIST (Wiener Osterstrietzel)

3/4 cup milk
1 cup butter
3/4 cup sugar
1/2 tsp. salt
2 pkg. active dry yeast
1/2 cup warm water
1 tsp. grated lemon peel
2 eggs
1 egg, separated
5-1/2 cups all-purpose flour
3/4 cup chopped filberts or slivered blanched almonds
granulated sugar

138

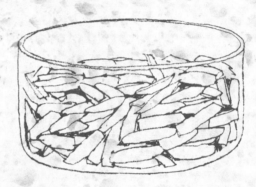

  Heat milk and butter until butter melts. Pour into a large mixing bowl with sugar and salt. Cool to lukewarm. Sprinkle yeast into warm water and let stand until dissolved. Stir into milk mixture. Beat in lemon peel, eggs, and egg yolk. Gradually add 3 cups flour and beat 5 minutes. Add enough remaining flour to make a soft dough. Beat with a heavy duty electric mixer or wooden spoon. Mix in 1/2 cup nuts. Turn out onto a lightly floured board and knead until smooth and satiny. Place in a greased bowl. Butter top of dough lightly. Cover with a clean kitchen towel and let rise in a warm place until doubled in size. Turn out on a floured board and knead lightly. Cut off 1/3 of the dough. Divide remaining dough into 3 strips, each about 18 inches long, and braid. Place on a greased baking sheet. Divide the smaller piece of dough into 3 strips and braid. Place on top of the larger braid. Cover with a towel and let rise in a warm place until almost doubled in size. Beat egg white until foamy and brush over top and sides of loaf. Sprinkle with granulated sugar and remaining nuts. Bake in 350° F oven 45 to 50 minutes, or until golden brown and loaf sounds hollow when thumped. Place on a cake rack. To serve, cut in slices and serve warm or cool. Makes 1 large loaf.

CZECHOSLOVAKIAN VANOCKA

Pronounced 'von-ooch-kah'. For Christmas it is traditionally shaped in a three-tiered braided loaf. You may make smaller ones if desired.

1 pkg. active dry yeast
1/4 cup warm water
2 eggs
1 egg, separated
6 tbs. sugar
1/2 cup butter
1 cup milk

1/2 tsp. salt
2 tsp. grated lemon peel
4-1/2 to 5 cups all-purpose flour
1/2 cup golden raisins
1/2 cup slivered blanched almonds
Lemon Glaze, page 141

140

Sprinkle yeast into warm water. Let stand until dissolved. In a large mixing bowl, beat whole eggs and egg yolk until blended. Stir in sugar. Heat butter and milk until warm. Add to egg mixture. Blend in salt, lemon peel and dissolved yeast. Gradually add enough flour to make a soft dough. Mix in raisins and almonds. Turn out onto a lightly floured board. Knead until smooth. Place in a greased bowl. Butter top of dough lightly. Cover with a clean kitchen towel. Let rise in a warm place until doubled in size, about 1-1/2 hours. Punch dough down. Turn out on floured board and knead lightly. Divide in half. Divide one half in four pieces. Roll each into strands about 18 inches long. Braid the four strands. To do this lay out lengthwise. Pinch strands together at one end. Lift the right strand over the next one, under the third, and over the fourth. Repeat until all strands are braided. Tuck ends under at the finish. Divide the remaining dough in the following manner. Take two-thirds of the dough and divide into three pieces. Make strands about 16 inches long and braid. Place on top of the four strand braid. Divide remaining dough in half. Make two strands, each about 14 inches long. Twist these together and place on top. Transfer to a greased baking sheet. Cover with a towel and let rise until doubled in size, about 45 minutes. Beat remaining egg white until light and brush over top. Bake in 350° F oven 35 to 40 minutes or until golden brown and loaf sounds hollow when thumped. Transfer to a cake rack to cool slightly. Spread with Lemon Glaze while still warm.

Lemon Glaze: Blend 1 cup powdered sugar with 2 teaspoons <u>each</u> lemon juice and milk. Use as directed. Makes 1 large braid.

PUEBLO FESTIVAL BREAD

New Mexico Indians bake this fanciful white bread in their beehive-shaped, outdoor ovens especially for festival days. Pull it apart for easy serving.

4 cups all-purpose flour
1 pkg. active dry yeast
2 tsp. salt
2 tbs. soft butter
1 tbs. sugar
1-1/2 cups very warm water (125°)

142

Place 1-1/2 cups flour, the yeast, salt, butter and sugar in a mixing bowl. Pour in warm water and beat 2 minutes. Gradually add remaining flour, beating with a heavy duty electric mixer or wooden spoon. Turn out on a floured board and knead until smooth and satiny and no longer sticky. Place in a greased bowl. Butter top of dough lightly and cover with a clean kitchen towel. Let rise in a warm place until doubled in size. Punch dough down and turn out on lightly floured board. Knead again to remove air bubbles. Divide dough into two equal pieces. With a rolling pin, roll each into a flat cake about 8 inches in diameter. Place in greased 9-inch pie pans. Then fold each in half, bringing the top half to within 1/2 inch of the bottom edge. With a sharp knife slash loaf twice about 2/3 of the way through the loaf on the rounded side making 3 equal sections. Spread the slashed sections about 1 inch apart. Cover with a towel and let rise in a warm place until doubled in size. Bake in 350° F oven 35 minutes or until golden brown and loaves sound hollow when thumped. Makes 2 loaves.

143

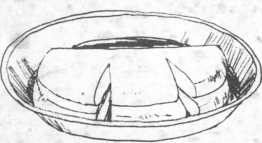

ORNAMENTAL WREATH

A braided wreath of bread adds a festive touch to a holiday kitchen. Decorate with ornamental fruit or mushrooms and tie with a bright bow and a sheaf of grain. This ornamental wreath keeps nicely from year to year.

1 pkg. active dry yeast
1-1/4 cups warm water
1 tbs. sugar
2 tbs. salad oil
1 tsp. salt
4 cups all-purpose flour
1 egg white, lightly beaten

Sprinkle yeast into warm water in a large mixing bowl. Let stand until dissolved. Mix in sugar, oil and salt. Gradually add enough flour to make a stiff dough. Turn out on a floured board and knead thoroughly, about 10 minutes. Place in a greased bowl. Butter top of dough lightly. Cover and let

rise in a warm place until doubled. Punch down and let rise again until doubled. Turn out on a floured board and knead lightly. Divide into 3 pieces. Roll into strands about 25 inches long. Braid and bring ends together forming a wreath. Place on a greased baking sheet. Let rise 20 minutes. Brush with egg white. Bake in a 425° F oven 10 minutes. Reduce heat to 300° F and bake 1 hour longer or until loaf is dry throughout. Let cool and decorate. Makes 1 wreath.

Dessert Breads

BUNDT COFFEECAKE

Chocolate streusel swirls inside this tender decorative fluted coffeecake.

1 pkg. active dry yeast	1/2 cup sour cream
1/4 cup warm water	2/3 cup butter
1/2 cup sugar	3 cups all-purpose flour
2 egg yolks	2 tbs. melted butter
1/2 tsp. salt	Chocolate Streusel
1 tsp. vanilla	Orange Glaze: 1 cup powdered sugar
1/4 cup milk	blended with 4 tsp. orange juice.

148

Sprinkle yeast into warm water in a large mixing bowl. Let stand until dissolved. Add sugar, egg yolks, salt and vanilla. Heat milk and sour cream to lukewarm. Stir into yeast mixture. Cut butter into 2-1/2 cups flour until the mixture has a coarse crumb-like consistency. Add to yeast mixture and stir until blended. Gradually add remaining flour, mixing until smooth. Turn out onto floured board and knead a few minutes until dough is smooth and no longer sticky. Place in a greased bowl. Butter top of dough lightly and cover with a kitchen towel. Let rise until doubled in size, about 1-1/2 hours. Punch dough down. Turn out onto floured board and knead lightly. Roll out into a rectangle about 12 x 16 inches. Spread with melted butter and sprinkle with Chocolate Streusel. Roll up like a jelly roll. Place seam side up in a greased 9 or 10-inch bundt or tube pan. Cover with a kitchen towel and let rise in a warm place until doubled in size, about 45 minutes. Bake in 350° F oven 45 to 50 minutes, or until loaf sounds hollow when thumped. Let cool on cake rack a few minutes, then remove from pan. While still warm drizzle top of loaf with Orange Glaze. Makes 1 large coffeecake.

149

  Chocolate Streusel: Mix together until crumbly 2 tablespoons each butter and flour, 1/2 cup brown sugar and 1 tablespoon unsweetened cocoa.

GERMAN HONEY BEE CAKE (Bienenstich)

A caramelized, toasted almond topping glazes this tender coffeecake.

1/3 cup milk
1/3 cup butter
1/4 cup sugar
1/2 tsp. salt
1 pkg. active dry yeast
1/4 cup warm water
2-1/2 cups all-purpose flour
1 egg
1 egg yolk
1 tsp. grated lemon peel
Almond Topping

150

Heat milk and butter until very warm. Pour over sugar and salt in a large mixing bowl. Cool to lukewarm. Sprinkle yeast into warm water and let stand until dissolved. Add to milk mixture. Beat in 1 cup flour until smooth. Add egg and egg yolk. Beat until smooth. Stir in lemon peel. Gradually add enough flour to make a soft dough. Turn dough out onto floured board and knead until smooth. Place in a greased bowl and butter top of dough lightly. Cover with a clean kitchen towel and let rise in a warm place until doubled in size, about 1-1/2 hours. Punch dough down. Turn out onto floured board and knead lightly. Roll into a 10-inch circle. Fit into a greased 10-inch spring-form pan. Cover and let rise until doubled in size, about 40 minutes. Bake in 350° F oven 15 minutes. Spread Almond Topping carefully on top. Bake 15 minutes longer or until nicely browned. Cool on rack and slice. Makes 1 large loaf. 151

Almond Topping: Place 1/3 cup brown sugar and 2 tablespoons each honey, butter and heavy cream in saucepan. Bring to a boil. Boil until thickened, about 3 minutes. Add 3/4 cup sliced almonds. Use as directed.

SAVARIN WITH FRUIT

This liqueur-drenched cake ring is enhanced by juicy strawberries and sweetened whipped cream. It makes a festive party dessert.

1 pkg. active dry yeast
1/4 cup warm water
1/2 cup butter
1/3 cup sugar
4 egg yolks
1 tsp. grated lemon peel

1 tsp. vanilla
2 cups all-purpose flour
1/2 cup warm milk
Liqueur Syrup, page 153
strawberries
sweetened whipped cream

152

Sprinkle yeast into warm water and let stand until dissolved. Cream butter. Beat in sugar and egg yolks. Add lemon peel, vanilla, dissolved yeast and 1 cup flour. Beat until smooth. Add warm milk. Beat until smooth. Blend in remaining 1 cup flour and beat 5 minutes longer. Heavily butter a 2-quart, 9-inch tube pan (preferably one with a fluted design). Spoon in batter. Cover with a towel. Place in a warm spot and let rise until tripled in size. Bake in 350° F oven 40 minutes, or until a wooden skewer inserted in the center comes out clean. Place on cake rack to cool in pan 5 minutes. With a skewer, prick cake. Spoon cooled syrup over the cake. Cool in pan. To serve, turn cake ring out onto a platter. Fill center with berries. Accompany with a bowl of whipped cream. Makes about 12 servings.

Liqueur Syrup: Combine 1 cup sugar, 1 cup water and 1 teaspoon lemon peel in a saucepan. Boil, stirring, just until sugar is dissolved. Remove from heat. Add 1/4 cup <u>each</u> brandy or Cognac and an orange-flavored liqueur. Use as directed.

RUM BABA

Follow the recipe for Savarin With Fruit except add 1/3 cup currants, plumped in Madeira or medium dry sherry, to the batter before spooning it into the pan. Make Liqueur Syrup using 1/2 cup rum, instead of brandy and the orange-flavored liqueur, and any excess Madeira or sherry left from plumping the currants. Pour over cake as directed.

CRISS-CROSS COFFEE CAKE

You fill and shape this loaf on the baking sheet by criss crossing the cut strips of dough.

1 pkg. active dry yeast
1/4 cup warm water
2 eggs
1/2 cup sugar
1/2 tsp. salt
1 tsp. vanilla extract
1/4 cup sour cream
6 tbs. melted butter, cooled
2-1/2 cups all-purpose flour
Nut Filling, page 156
1 egg white, lightly beaten
sugar for topping
sliced almonds

154

Sprinkle yeast into warm water and let stand until dissolved. In a large mixing bowl, beat eggs until light. Gradually beat in sugar, salt, vanilla, sour cream and butter. Add 1-1/2 cups flour and beat 5 minutes longer. Beat in remaining flour using a heavy duty electric mixer or wooden spoon. Turn dough out onto floured board and knead 5 minutes. Place in greased bowl and butter top of dough lightly. Cover with a clean kitchen towel and let rise in a

155

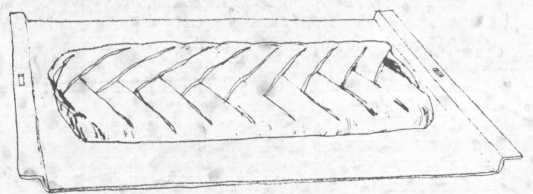

continued

warm place until doubled in size. Punch dough down and turn out on a floured board. Roll into a rectangle about 10 x 15 inches. Lay on a lightly greased baking sheet. Mark dough into three equal lengthwise sections. Spread filling on the center third of the dough. With a sharp knife, cut diagonal strips 1 inch apart on each of the outer two sections of dough, cutting almost to filling. Overlap strips first from one side, then the other. Brush loaf with beaten egg white. Sprinkle with sugar and about 2 tablespoons sliced almonds. Cover with a towel and let rise until doubled. Bake in 350° F oven 30 minutes, or until golden brown. Makes 1 loaf.

156   Nut Filling: Beat 1 egg until light. Beat in 1/2 cup firmly packed brown sugar, 3/4 cup ground almonds or filberts (lightly toasted, if desired) and 3/4 cup sponge cake or sugar cooky crumbs. Use as directed.

Alternate Prune, Apricot or Date Filling: Combine 1-1/4 cups dried pitted prunes, apricots, or dates, 1 cup water, 1/3 cup honey and 1 teaspoon grated lemon peel. Bring to a boil. Cook, covered, 10 to 12 minutes or until tender and liquid is absorbed. Let cool. Use as directed.

CHEESE-FILLED COFFEE RING

Sour cream sweet bread rings the cheesecake center of this Hungarian innovation.

1 pkg. active dry yeast	1/4 tsp. salt
1/4 cup warm water	2-1/2 cups all-purpose flour
1/2 cup butter	2 pkg. (3 oz. ea.) cream cheese
3 egg yolks	1 egg
2/3 cup sugar	1/2 tsp. vanilla
1/2 cup sour cream	1/2 cup apricot jam

Sprinkle yeast into warm water and let stand until dissolved. Melt butter. In a large mixing bowl beat egg yolks until thick and light. Blend in 1/3 cup sugar, sour cream, melted butter and salt. Stir in dissolved yeast. Gradually stir in the flour, mixing to make a smooth, soft dough. Turn out onto a floured board and knead 5 minutes. Place in a greased bowl. Butter top of dough lightly and cover with a clean kitchen towel. Let rise in a warm place until almost doubled in size, about 1-1/2 hours. To make filling, beat cream cheese (warmed to room temperature) with remaining 1/3 cup sugar and egg. Blend in vanilla. Punch the dough down and turn out onto a floured board. Knead a few minutes. Roll dough into a circle about 15 inches in diameter. Lay the dough over a greased 1-1/2-quart ring mold. Fit the dough carefully down into the bottom and sides of the mold. Be careful not to poke holes in it. Let it hang over the outside. Pour in the cheese filling. Lift outside edges of dough and lap over filling. Seal to inside ring of dough. Cut a cross in the dough which covers the center hole of ring mold. Fold each triangle formed back over the ring. Cover with a towel and let rise in a warm place until doubled in size, about 45 minutes. Bake in 350° F oven 30 to 35 minutes, or until golden brown. Let cool 10 minutes, then turn out with top side down. When cool, heat jam until it flows easily. Force through a wire sieve. Spoon over ring. Cut into wedges. Makes 1 bread ring.

159

Cheese-Filled Coffee Ring pictured on page 157.

HONEY-GLAZED SPIRAL BREAD

A caramelized sheath of crunchy nuts bakes on this pinwheel of sweet bread.

1 pkg. active dry yeast
1/4 cup warm water
6 tbs. butter
2/3 cup sugar
1/2 tsp. salt
1 tsp. grated orange peel
3 eggs
1 cup lukewarm milk
4 cups all-purpose flour
Honey Glaze
1/2 cup chopped walnuts or slivered almonds

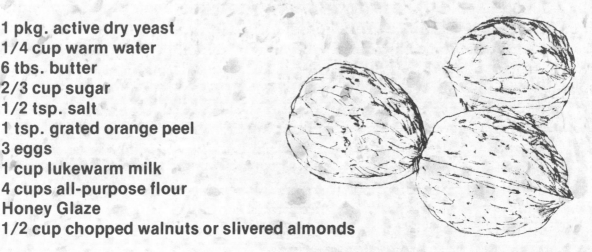

Stir yeast into warm water and let stand until dissolved. Cream butter and sugar in a large mixing bowl. Beat in salt, orange peel, eggs and milk. Blend in dissolved yeast. Add 1 cup flour and beat until smooth. Add 1-1/2 cups flour and beat 5 minutes. Gradually add enough remaining flour to make a soft dough. Turn out on a lightly floured board and knead until smooth and satiny, about 5 to 10 minutes. Place in a greased bowl. Lightly butter the top of the dough. Cover, and let rise in a warm place until doubled in size. Turn dough out and knead lightly on a floured board. Divide dough in half. Using finger tips, roll each piece into a long rope about 1 inch thick. Place on a greased baking sheet and coil into a spiral. Repeat with remaining dough. Cover and let rise in a warm place until doubled in size. Spread surface with Honey Glaze and sprinkle with nuts. Bake in a 350° F oven 35 minutes, or until golden brown. Serve warm. Makes 2 spirals.

Honey Glaze: Beat together until smooth 2 tablespoons soft butter, 3/4 cup powdered sugar, 2 tablespoons honey, and 1 egg white. Use as directed.

VERONA LOAF

This lemon-scented Italian loaf calls for rolling and folding firm butter slices into the dough. The result is a lovely tender loaf with buttery pockets throughout.

3-1/4 cups all-purpose flour
1/3 cup sugar
1/2 tsp. salt
1 tbs. grated lemon peel
1 pkg. active dry yeast
3/4 cup very warm water (125°)
1/2 cup butter
3 eggs
1-1/2 tsp. vanilla extract
1 egg white, lightly beaten
granulated sugar for topping

continued

Place 1 cup flour, sugar, salt, lemon peel and yeast in a large mixing bowl. Gradually add very warm water and beat until smooth. Beat in 1/4 cup butter, cut in small pieces. Beat at medium speed for 2 minutes. Add eggs, vanilla and 1/2 cup flour. Beat hard 2 minutes longer. Gradually add enough remaining flour to make a soft dough. Turn dough out onto lightly floured board and knead until smooth and satiny. Place in a greased bowl and butter the top of dough lightly. Cover with a clean kitchen towel and let rise in a warm place until doubled in size, about 45 minutes. Punch dough down and turn out onto floured board. Knead lightly and roll into a rectangle about 1/2 inch thick. Cut 2 tablespoons butter into small pieces. Place in center 1/3 of the dough. Fold 1/3 of the dough over the butter and place remaining butter, cut in pieces, on top. Bring remaining 1/3 of dough over to cover butter. Roll out making a strip 18 inches long. Fold into thirds and wrap loosely in waxed paper. Refrigerate 20 minutes. Repeat, rolling dough into 18 inch strip, folding into thirds and chilling 2 times. On a floured board divide dough in half. Stretch the top of each piece, pulling it underneath to form a ball. Place in two greased 8-inch round cake pans. Cover and let rise in a warm place until doubled in size, about 35 minutes. Brush with lightly beaten egg white and sprinkle with sugar. Bake in 350° F oven 30 to 35 minutes, or until loaves sound hollow when thumped. Remove from pans and cool slightly. Serve warm with sweet butter. Makes 2 loaves.

FRENCH GALETTE (Dessert Tart Perouges Style)

This big pizza-like sweet bread makes a spectacular dessert. Serve it piping hot from the oven, short-cake style, with fresh berries and cream.

1 pkg. active dry yeast
6 tbs. warm water
1/2 cup soft butter
10 tbs. sugar
1 egg
1 tsp. grated lemon peel
166 1/2 tsp. salt
1-3/4 cups all-purpose flour

Sprinkle yeast into warm water in a large mixing bowl and let stand until dissolved. Beat in 1/4 cup butter, 2 tablespoons sugar, egg, lemon peel and salt. Gradually add enough flour to make a soft dough. Beat well. Turn out dough onto floured board and knead until satiny and no longer sticky. Place in a greased bowl and butter top of dough lightly. Cover with a clean kitchen towel and let rise in a warm place until doubled in size. Punch dough down and turn out onto floured board. Knead lightly. Roll out into a 15-inch circle and place in greased 14-inch pizza pan or on baking sheet. Form a rim around the edge. Spread with remaining 1/4 cup soft butter and sprinkle with remaining 1/4 cup sugar. Let stand in a warm place 20 minutes. Bake in 500° F oven 6 minutes or until golden brown. Serve at once, hot, cut into pie-shaped wedges. If desired, accompany with vanilla-flavored whipped cream or ice cream and fresh berries or sliced peaches. Makes 8 servings.

167

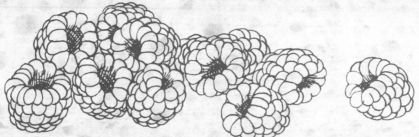

CHOCOLATE LOAVES

Here is a bread for chocolate lovers.

1 pkg. active dry yeast
1/4 cup warm water
1-3/4 cups milk, heated to lukewarm
1/2 cup butter
3/4 cup sugar
3 eggs
5 cups all-purpose flour
1/2 cup unsweetened cocoa
1 tsp. _each_ salt and vanilla extract
3/4 cup chopped walnuts _or_ pecans
Powdered Sugar Glaze

Sprinkle yeast into warm water and let stand until dissolved. Cream butter in large mixing bowl. Beat in sugar and eggs. Stir in milk and dissolved yeast.

Add 2 cups flour and beat until smooth. Mix in cocoa, salt and vanilla. Add enough remaining flour to make a soft dough. Stir in nuts. Turn out onto lightly floured board and knead until smooth and satiny. Place in a greased bowl and butter top of dough lightly. Cover with a clean kitchen towel and let rise in a warm place until doubled in size. Turn dough out onto lightly floured board and knead until smooth. Divide in half and shape into two round loaves. Place in greased 8 or 9-inch round cake pans. Cover with a towel and let rise in a warm place until doubled in size, about 45 minutes. Bake in 350° F oven 35 to 40 minutes or until loaves sound hollow when thumped. Remove from pans and let cool on cake rack. Spread with Powdered Sugar Glaze. Makes 2 round loaves.

Powdered Sugar Glaze: Beat together 1-1/2 cups powdered sugar, 1-1/2 tablespoons milk, and 1 teaspoon vanilla or rum. Use as directed.

Sourdough Breads

171

SOURDOUGH STARTER

The zesty sourdough flavor of bread is achieved by a "starter". Several are available commercially or you may create your own. Success is not guaranteed with either, as sometimes the microorganisims simply don't respond with their characteristic sourdough flavor and leavening potential. When the starter does produce at its optimum, the results are outstanding.

2 cups lukewarm water (110°)   2 cups all-purpose flour
1 pkg. active dry yeast   1/2 tsp. salt

172   Combine the water and yeast in a medium-sized crock or bowl and let stand until dissolved. Blend in flour and salt. Cover loosely with cheesecloth and place in a warm spot (ideally 80°). Each day for 4 days add 1/2 cup lukewarm water and 1/2 cup flour to feed the starter. At the end of 4 to 6 days, it should begin to give off a sour smell. Cover tightly and refrigerate. As you use the starter, replace it with equal amounts of lukewarm water and flour. It should be fed at least once a week by adding additional water and flour.

SOURDOUGH BAGUETTES

Long slender French baguettes offer lots of crusty sour dough goodness.

1 cup lukewarm water
1 tbs. sugar
2 tbs. melted butter <u>or</u> salad oil
1 tbs. salt

1 cup sourdough starter
1/2 tsp. baking soda
4-1/2 cups all-purpose flour
1 egg white, lightly beaten

Stir water, sugar, butter and salt together in a mixing bowl. Mix in starter and soda. Gradually beat in enough flour to make a stiff dough. Turn out on a lightly floured board and knead until smooth and satiny. Place in a greased bowl. Cover. Let rise in a warm place until doubled in size. Turn out on a lightly floured board and knead lightly. Divide into 3 pieces. Roll each into a long thin roll, about 2 inches in diameter. Place on a greased baking sheet. Cover and let rise until doubled. Slash the surface diagonally with a sharp knife or a razor blade and brush with egg white. Bake at 375° F for 30 to 35 minutes or until golden brown and loaves sound hollow when thumped. Makes 3 loaves.

SOURDOUGH WHOLE WHEAT BREAD

Sourdough tang permeates this wholesome whole grain bread.

1 pkg. active dry yeast
3 cups unsifted whole wheat flour
4 cups all-purpose flour
1 cup <u>each</u> milk and water
3/4 cup sourdough starter
1/4 cup honey
1 tbs. salt
3 tbs. soft butter
1 tsp. soda

174

Place yeast, 1 cup whole wheat flour and 1 cup all-purpose flour in a large mixing bowl. Heat milk and water to 125°. Add to dry ingredients. Stir until blended. Mix in the starter and beat 5 minutes. Cover bowl with plastic film. Let stand in a warm place until bubbly, about 1-1/2 to 2 hours. Stir in honey, salt, butter and soda. Gradually mix in remaining wholewheat flour and enough all-purpose flour to make a stiff dough. Turn out on a floured board and knead until smooth. Place dough in a greased bowl. Cover and let rise in a warm place until doubled in size. Punch down and turn out on a floured board. Knead lightly. Divide in half and shape into loaves. Place in greased 9 x 5-inch loaf pans. Cover and let rise in a warm place until almost doubled in size. Bake in a 375° F oven 35 minutes or until loaves sound hollow when tapped. Remove from pans and let cool on cake racks. Makes 2 loaves.

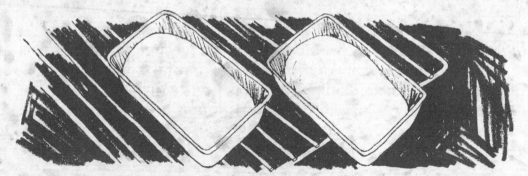

SOURDOUGH ENGLISH MUFFINS

These cornmeal-coated muffins are baked on a griddle until golden brown.

1 cup sourdough starter
2 cups milk
4-1/2 cups all-purpose flour
2 tbs. sugar
1-1/2 tsp. salt
1 tsp. soda
cornmeal

In a large mixing bowl combine starter, milk and 4 cups flour. Mix well with a wooden spoon. Cover loosely and let stand at room temperature 8 hours or overnight. Mix together remaining 1/2 cup flour with sugar, salt and soda. Sprinkle over dough and mix in. Turn stiff dough out onto a floured board. Knead a few minutes or until no longer sticky. Roll out dough 3/4 inch thick. Cut into rounds with a 3 inch cutter. Place 1 inch apart on a baking sheet sprinkled with cornmeal. Dust more cornmeal on top. Cover and let rise in a warm place until doubled. Bake on a lightly greased griddle at 275° F 8 to 10 minutes on a side. Turning once. Serve warm or split and toast. Makes about 2 dozen muffins.

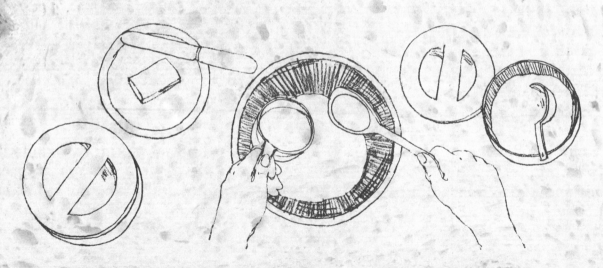

SOURDOUGH PANCAKES

Start these pancakes the night before so they'll be ready to bake the next morning. Honey-butter or berry jam make great toppings.

1/2 cup sourdough starter
2 cups milk
2 cups all-purpose flour
2 eggs
2 tbs. sugar
1/2 tsp. salt
1 tsp. soda

178

Combine starter, milk and flour in a large mixing bowl. Mix until blended. Cover and let stand in a warm place 8 hours, or overnight. Add eggs, sugar, salt and soda. Beat until blended. Pour batter into 3 inch cakes on a lightly greased, hot griddle. Cook until golden brown on both sides. Makes about 2-1/2 dozen pancakes.

JIM'S SOURDOUGH ROLLS

Here the basic pancake batter is the starting point for feather-light, butter-dipped rolls.

Prepare basic Sourdough Pancake batter as directed above. Mix in 1 teaspoon salt and enough flour (approximately 2-1/2 to 3 cups) to make a stiff dough. Turn out on a floured board and knead until smooth. Place in a greased bowl. Cover. Let rise until doubled in size. Turn dough onto a board and roll out about 3/4 inch thick. Cut out with a biscuit cutter and dip each roll in melted butter. Place in a greased pan, about 1 inch apart. Cover and let rise until doubled in size. Bake in a 375° F oven 25 to 30 minutes, or until golden brown. Makes about 3 dozen rolls.

179

Index

These lines from "The Rubaiyat" of Omar Khayyam, a Persian astronomer/poet from the 12th century, reveal the importance of bread in that era...

"Here with a loaf of bread beneath the bough,
A flask of wine, a book of verse—and Thou
Beside me singing in the wilderness—
And wilderness is paradise enow"